Praise for *Personal Energy Management*:

"The outline of the book is practical and easy to follow. In a world of quick-fixes and trendiness, Schultz places his reflections squarely in the long and tested tradition of Christian spirituality. The perennial wisdom of busy and productive Christians of every era shines through every section of this handbook. I can imagine Paul the Apostle reading this . . . Augustine . . . Thomas Aquinas . . . Theresa of Avila.

The management of human energy is an integral process. . . . Schultz insists on 'little victories' as essential to genuine development, [yet he] does not shy away from the central mystery of suffering in human experience.

Schultz's use of personal experience is restrained and judicious. [His] sense of humor is delightful and subtly playful. . . .

Because of the richness of this handbook and its thoroughness, it would be especially helpful to so many who strive to make a difference in life, in the world, in family, in parish, in ministries of all kinds."

Rev. Timothy Fitzgerald, C.P., S.T.D.
Itinerant Preacher and Retreat Coordinator

"This is not a 'quick fix' as often proposed by other human development authors. Rather, Mr. Schultz invites us to first increase our self-awareness, then develop new patterns that move toward realizing our full potential. . . . Anyone investing time in his book should reap benefits many times over—personally as well as professionally."

Diane M. Fletcher, R.N., M.A., B.S.N.
Pittsburgh Cancer Institute

"*Personal Energy Management* allows us to embark on a deep and meaningful journey inside of our personal and professional lives and our relationship with God to re-discover the purpose of our very being as Christians and business and professional people."

Laura M. Magone, M.B.A,
Small Business Development Center
Duquesne University

"Karl Schultz offers a quality interactive text that enables any-one, novice or otherwise, to engage serious questions at their own pace. In a certain sense this workbook sets up a gentle oscillation between questions in the text and response in the individual's life-text, which will enable growth, both personal and professional. My most consistently challenging ministry is spiritual direction, and I have found that the kind of questions in *Personal Energy Management* must be asked of any-one who takes seriously a commitment to Christ in prayer and in ministry."

Rev. Andrew S. Campbell, O.S.B., Ph.D.
St. Vincent Archabbey, Junior Master;
St. Vincent College, Communication
Program director

"Mr. Schultz is continually searching for paths of Christian peace in the midst of the hectic pressures of life. In *Personal Energy Management* he offers down to earth, concrete ways of living our real lives reflectively. He is convincing in show-ing that the 'Kingdom of God is not far from us' if only we live with hope in the Providence of God and a consciousness of inner strengths that can transform our way of living. It is not a question of control, but of consciousness: not a ques-tion of new techniques, but of discovering or rediscovering the inner gifts we already have."

Fr. Robert L. McCreary, O.F.M. Cap.
Novice Director, St. Conrad's Friary

"Schultz has written a beautiful Christian manual intended for those of us not interested in ruling the world but truly in need of ruling ourselves. The Reflection Exercises and other workbook sections provide the opportunity to individualize his excellent advice and thus use his manual over and over again as we continue our own growth journey toward God."

William A. Goyette, Attorney-at-Law

Personal Energy Management

Personal Energy Management

A Christian Personal and Professional Growth Program and Workbook

Karl A. Schultz

A Campion Book

Loyola University Press
Chicago

Loyola University Press
3441 North Ashland Avenue
Chicago, Illinois 60657

Library of Congress Cataloging-in-Publication data

Schultz, Karl A., 1959–
    Personal energy management: a Christian personal and professional
growth program and workbook / Karl A. Schultz.
        p.   cm.
    Includes bibliographical references.
    ISBN 0-8294-0807-X (alk. paper)
    1. Self-actualization (Psychology)—Religious aspects—Christianity. I. Title.
BV4598.2.S38   1994
248.4—dc20   94-25054
                                                                 CIP

To Jo-Ann—
my wife, helper, and partner—
with all my love always and forever.
Karl

Contents

Personal Energy Management *P* Parameters

Preface

I began our organization, Genesis Personal Development Center, and this book with the belief that authentic human development and achievement is the fruit of a balanced integration of mental, emotional, physical, and spiritual capacities in dialogue with God's people and Word. The values, traditions, and wisdom maxims of both the Jewish and Christian communities predate the human potential movement by millenniums, and provide a context and criteria for evaluating the movement's various developments and strains. This book is an attempt to integrate and develop the many complementary principles and practices of Christian spirituality and human development.

Little Victories

Because sincerity and hard work do not guarantee material or tangible results according to our desires and timetables, we must learn to recognize, appreciate, enjoy, and build upon the little victories and subtle opportunities that arise during our life journey. The concept of little victories is as valid for groups, families, relationships, and organizations as it is for individuals. In most human endeavors and challenges—including the dimensions of mind, body, and spirit—the healthiest and most enduring progress comes piecemeal. Forced, overnight changes in individuals, groups, or organizations can do violence to people and processes. Immediate and dramatic improvements are rare, generally circumstantial, and frequently short-lived. Children must learn to stand up before they can walk.

The principle underlying little victories is that growth and healing have their own timetables. We cooperate with the process by accumulating both related and diverse little victories. Their subtle, nonthreatening qualities disarm both internal and external opposition, and enable us to focus on the present and the possible.

Because the process of human growth and achievement is fundamentally continuous, we must find joy and fulfillment along the way as well as at the destination. In recognition of this, each chapter concludes with space for the reader to record some of their little victories of either a personal or professional nature. These little victories can also be recorded in a personal journal.

The Misleading Appeal of Instant and Easy Answers

Perhaps the most common temptation that personal development authors and speakers succumb to is that of oversimplification and excessive use of generalities and prospective rewards for the purpose of motivating their audience. Too often personal growth and motivation seminars lapse into rah-rah sessions and materialistic revival meetings in which psychological and pragmatic strategies overshadow fundamental moral, spiritual, and philosophical issues. Confidence, hope, and enthusiasm are essential qualities, but they must be balanced by sober recognition of the painful aspects of growth and life.

While motivational speakers and books correctly exhort us not to become overwhelmed by our impediments and perceived limitations, they often fail to caution us against moving toward the other extreme of denial and avoidance of our problems. Our attention and energy should be directed toward finding workable ways to live with legitimate limitations while making the best of the wonderful gifts and possibilities that God and life offer us. We must allow for and be prepared to deal with the uncertainty and perplexing inconsistencies and injustices of life.

Many human potential advocates oversimplify the challenge of coping with the pain and imperfection of life by suggesting that changes can be made easily and overnight. Rather than promote ambitious life-changing strategies and dramatic personal transformations, I prefer to focus on attaining little victories. Development of mind, body, and spirit is healthiest and most enduring when procured gradually and with an understanding of the roots of our dilemmas and weaknesses.

The energizing and motivational potential of little victories helps us cope and grow through our peaks and valleys. We could apply this coping and growth concept to each topic or *P* parameter discussed in the book, and ask what little victories are within reach on a daily basis. Before we know it, we will have compiled an impressive array of accomplishments that elude the opposition of naysayers and our own internal defense systems.

Integrity

While integrity is a perennial staple of human development discussions, it is often overlooked that *integrity* has a linguistic relationship in Hebrew to *wellness, wholeness,* and *completeness*. Integrity is a personal commitment in word and deed to core beliefs and values. We must not confuse integrity with perfection or innocence, for the Scriptures tell us that even the just person falls seven times a day. Life's bumps and bruises can damage our reputation, self-image, and capacity on various levels to enjoy life, but they need not diminish our integrity. We alone can devalue or relinquish our integrity. Even when we compromise our integrity, we can always reclaim it through regret, reparation, and future resolve.

Human beings at their deepest level need to hear the truth. We may not be satisfied with life at any given moment, but we can still have some degree of inner peace. If we approach our quest with humor, patience, and humility, we can endure the bumps and enjoy the ride, and with affirmation and thanksgiving toward God, ourselves, and others, marvel at how far we have come.

* * *

Human development is an evolutionary art and science with both recognized and anonymous contributors. All personal effectiveness theories and models build on the efforts of others. I acknowledge my indebtedness to the countless persons, groups, and institutions known and unknown, past and present, who have influenced the shaping of this book. Its value lies not in its proposition of new truths, but in its affirmation, reformulation, and integration of timeless human values and principles into a cohesive and practical personal growth path.

Introduction

The *P* Parameters

M any of the values and practices that I recommend to the reader begin with the letter *P*. In the Personal Energy Management workshop, we refer to these as the *P parameters*. This alliteration helps us remember these building blocks as we immerse ourselves in the daily challenges of working and living.

How to Use This Book

Personal Energy Management consists of short chapters containing essays, exercises, and practical guidelines and pointers for personal growth. The book is divided into three parts: Personal Energy Management Principles, Practices, and Mismanagement Patterns. Each of these parts emphasizes the reader's participation through creative application and synthesis based on personal needs and circumstances. To facilitate this participation, each chapter concludes with exercises or guidelines designed to stimulate reflection and practical responses. Space is provided at the end of each chapter for readers to record their own reflections, applications, and little victories. My hope is that by integrating introspection and practical applications, readers will derive helpful insights into their personal and professional situations.

This book is designed to be read reflectively and with flexibility. While its depth, comprehensiveness, and progression make it a suitable text for high school, college, and adult religion or human development courses, the stand-alone quality of its chapters serves the purpose of individuals interested in particular personal growth topics. The more pressing our need for growth in a specific area, the more time and energy we should devote to it. A particular sentence or paragraph may inspire insights and applications sufficient for our reading period. So be it; basic principles can have complex and comprehensive applications.

Information on the Personal Energy Management workshop, daily time and activity planner *(Personal Energy Manager)*, and audiocassettes that complement the book can be obtained by contacting Genesis Personal Development Center at the following address and telephone number:

Genesis Personal Development Center
P.O. Box 201
Glenshaw, Pennsylvania 15116
(412) 486-6087

* * *

You will find that inclusive language is not used in this book. The masculine singular pronoun and possessive adjective are used solely to maintain consistency. I ask your forbearance on this sensitive issue, and encourage any mental insertions or modifications that seem appropriate.

Part One

Foundations of Personal Energy Management
The *P* Principles

1

Philosophy

Defining Personal Energy Management

Personal Energy Management is an approach to living and working that is rooted in traditional and timeless human wisdom. It makes no pretense of providing answers to life's ultimate questions, nor is it intended to be a comprehensive theory on the art of living. Personal Energy Management seeks to integrate and harmonize personal and professional development by channeling our efforts, emotions, capabilities, and energies in a creative manner. The word *energy* is used as a composite term for those controllable factors and capacities that God and human circumstances have placed in our hands. Energy works well as a symbol for our creative powers and resources because we instinctively know that we have only so much of it.

Personal Energy Management is rooted in the wisdom of what has come to be known as the "Serenity Prayer," composed by Reinhold Niebuhr and now a staple of the various twelve-step programs: "God give us the grace to accept with serenity the things that cannot be changed, courage to change the things that should be changed, and the wisdom to distinguish one from the other." Instead of trying to manipulate others, life, and even ourselves, why not simply try to manage what is within our control to the best of our ability? Anything more becomes too complicated and confusing. There are enough perplexing things in life.

What are the controllable variables of self-management? Chief among these are our abilities, emotions, actions, and perhaps most fundamentally, our energy. How easy it is to misdirect our attention and efforts due to misguided thinking, immature choices, and unrealistic expectations! Imagine working toward channeling our energies, abilities, and resources in productive ways. So much waste and heartache (sometimes literally) would be reduced or eliminated.

Personal Energy Management is the practice of managing ourselves and our situations, both at work and at home, within the limitations and possibilities that life presents to us. We direct our energies, abilities, and resources toward goals, values, and principles that are within our influence and realm of responsibility. Personal Energy Management is a straightforward concept grounded in common sense and human experience. The theory is simple, but the practice is difficult. In the succeeding chapters of this book, we discuss different aspects of Personal Energy Management as applied to both personal and professional endeavors and circumstances. As we learn and apply this approach as individuals, we can prudently share it with and apply it to our families, churches, companies, and organizations.

Affinities with Time and Stress Management

Personal Energy Management borrows many of its concepts from traditional methods of time and stress management, reformulating them based on its distinct philosophy and focus.

Our book and workshop on the topic of stress is entitled "Stress Transformation" rather than "Stress Management." The more we try to manage (that is, control and conform) stress in a grasping, desperate fashion, the more anxious and controlling we are tempted to become. Some stressors can be diminished or eliminated through logical analysis, psychological understanding, and creative responsibility, while other forms of stress cross over into the realm of suffering. This is where the Christian perspective transcends the capacity of humanistic psychology.

One of the fundamental messages of Scripture, tradition, and the living church is that suffering is a central part of life because it defines who we are in relationship to God, each other, and the natural and material world. Stress Transformation distinguishes between controllable stressors and legitimate suffering that contains elements beyond our control. It provides activities, values, and dispositions for taking a hopeful and proactive approach toward both controllable and uncontrollable stimuli and situations. Stress Transformation differs from Personal Energy Management, not in philosophy or values, but in objectives. Stress Transformation focuses primarily on health, balance, and wellness, while Personal Energy Management helps us think and behave effectively in everyday matters, and work toward our personal and professional potential.

The problem with time management in both theory and practice is that time is an elusive and relative dimension. It is utilized best by working and living in fidelity to our core beliefs, values, and principles, and using our resources of circumstance, talent, and treasure (material resources) to the best of our ability. In materialistic philosophies, time, achievement, and production take precedence over people issues. In Personal Energy Management, time is an important pragmatic element that supports, rather than supersedes, human values.

The more we are preoccupied with time, the less attention and energy we can devote to issues that are within our control. We must value and utilize time prudently without becoming obsessed with efficiency and immediate results. We should be interested in an effectiveness that is not measured solely in production, but in the quality of our being and relating as well. Sometimes this entails involving ourselves in activities and conversations that benefit others and overall long-term objectives, but do not contribute to our immediate ends.

From both a philosophical and a pragmatic standpoint, time exists outside of human beings. It marches on whether we like it or not. We cannot stop it, slow it down, or speed it up. Human experience of life is relative: When we are enjoying ourselves, time seems to fly, and when we are uncomfortable, it drags.

Personal Energy Management: A Support and Path, Not a Solution or Destination

Ultimately, Personal Energy Management is a humble approach to the art, science, and philosophy of practical human wisdom in subordination to the divine wisdom (cf. Jb 28). It is designed to help us progress in doing the fundamentals correctly, in unison, and in balance. God willing, our efforts will bear fruit in health, growth, and achievement. As we try to grow personally and professionally, we must not let any human system, philosophy, method, or technique, including Personal Energy Management, be an end in itself or a stumbling block in our call to live in fidelity to God's will and providence.

Reflection Exercises

Consider your approach to life in relation to Personal Energy Management. What are the similarities and differences?

Are there ways in which your attitudes and actions can be gradually and gently brought into conformity with the perspective of the "Serenity Prayer," changing what you can and leaving to providence what is beyond your control? What fruits might this yield?

Discuss your personal perspective/outlook on time. What values are operative? What are the mental and behavioral by-products of your current perspective?

Have there been times where you gave your time in the name of love and charity, rather than effectiveness, and been blessed? Have there been times where you felt burned and regretful? What can you learn from these experiences?

Are there ways in which you can balance and integrate the values of time, achievement, and success with the needs and dignity of yourself and others in a more healthy and loving way? We can reframe the question as follows: Do you value and approach being/living and doing/achieving with commensurate zest and respect?

Discuss how you might modify your philosophy and practical approach toward time and stressors. Visualize and describe the fruits of your new outlook and actions.

Reflections, Applications, and Little Victories

2

Prayer and Providence

In the context of Personal Energy Management, *prayer* and *providence* symbolize our status as relational beings who are not totally self-sufficient and independent. Personal effectiveness is a community affair; we need the help of others and God.

The personal and professional growth journey is intertwined with an understanding and experience of prayer and providence. A healthy attitude toward prayer and providence compels us to balance patient trust and receptivity with responsible action. Sometimes the struggle to be yourself and do your best becomes too intense, and it is necessary to lament your situation and petition God's assistance. I have experienced, during both good and bad times, what I have discerned as subtle signs of God's providence, which have provided me with hope and strength. There have also been occasions when I was angry and frustrated with God, and have not hesitated to tell him. It would be dishonest for me to talk about effectiveness without emphasizing two spiritual principles, prayer and providence, that have been foundational and pivotal in my own and many others' development.

Prayer

Prayer is dialogue with God or a higher power. Like all forms of human communication, it has both active and receptive elements. Because of its highly personal nature, and the theological and experiential issues that influence our approach to prayer, I will limit my comments to testifying to the importance of prayer in my own personal growth and achievement journey. I have turned to prayer in both good and bad times. It has not always provided answers, or even a sense of peace, but I believe God wants to dialogue with me, with my best interests in mind. Prayer is a good outlet for frustrations and inner toxins, as well as praise and thanksgiving. It supports and guides us, while helping regenerate the energy we need to persevere in our quests.

Providence

A belief in providence adds a spiritual confidence to our Personal Energy Management efforts. If we believe that behind the apparent chaos and madness of life there lies a mysterious purpose ordained and orchestrated by God in cooperation with human freedom, it will be easier for us to cope with negative experiences. A belief in providence reinforces Personal Energy Management through its expression of hope that good can and is being brought out of all human events. *Providence* is the divine energy in mysterious interaction with human freedom and events that directs the course of human history. On a practical note, faith in providence can provide a sense of peace and trust amid the confusion of daily life. It can help us not only on a spiritual level, but on a psychological, physiological, and pragmatic level as well. Trust in God and peace of mind help us avoid chronic anxiety, ulcers, and excessive and counter-productive efforts. We can direct our energies in a calm, purposeful manner.

Faith in providence is a characteristic of most of the people I have encountered who have survived tragic situations with a positive perspective. Without faith in providence, it is difficult to find redemptive value in suffering and stress. Prayer is a channel for reflecting on God's providential activity and initiative in our lives and the world, in both good and bad times. It compels us to unite our personal growth efforts with

God's will in a spirit of trust and hope, rather than resentment and fatalism.

___

Prayer and Providence:
The Gasoline and the Oil

Prayer is communication with God, not only in thoughts, words, and images, but in deeds as well. Living and acting with integrity is an essential fruit and aspect of prayer. *Providence* is the faith principle that God actively cares and provides for all creation, and that all things work together for the good of those who love God.

There is an automotive industry proverb that cars travel on gas, but run on oil. The car's dependence on gasoline is more urgent and obvious, but it is the oil that facilitates the smooth interaction of the engine and mechanical operations. Prayer is the gasoline of Personal Energy Management, and providence is the oil. The necessity, effects, and availability of prayer are more apparent, while providence manifests itself subtly and to the eyes of faith. Inordinate or insufficient attention to either creates problems: Insufficient oil, akin to trying to do everything by ourselves, burns and stresses the engine, or our body, mind, and spirit. Excessive amounts, akin to irresponsible dependence on providence, flood and smother the operations, or our efforts, and prevent us from hitting on all cylinders and realizing our potential. Insufficient gas/prayer drains the car/person of energy and motivation, while inordinate levels constitute a misdirection and misuse of resources. Balancing reliance on prayer and providence fosters a healthy tension between nature and grace, constituting a lifelong journey for which Personal Energy Management serves as a partial road map.

Prayer inspires and invigorates our efforts as we persist toward a worthy goal. Faith in providence offers a calmer and steadier ride than we would experience otherwise. Together they inspire us to work toward our potential in partnership and dialogue with God. Their complementary and interdependent nature is an article of faith. To paraphrase the maxim of Saint Ignatius of Loyola: Pray as if everything depends on God, act as if it depends on you. This paradoxical proverb captures the responsible yet interdependent nature of the human vocation and potential.

A Theological and Anthropological Foundation for Providence

As weak, vulnerable, and sinful human beings, there is inevitably a disparity between our beliefs, values, prayers, desires, and intentions, and our words and deeds. We try to manage our energies, abilities, and situations responsibly, prudently, morally, and creatively, and we fail as well as succeed. The mercy and redemptive suffering of Christ calls us to forgive ourselves and others for this aspect of the human condition and withhold judgment. We can admit that we are unwilling hypocrites, and ask God to help us learn and grow. As Paul laments in Rom 7:7–25, even our best efforts and intentions seem to go awry, and we inevitably fall on the mercy and providence of God. Sometimes our pride and self-deception causes us to forget this, and we set ourselves up for a fall. Thankfully, we can always get back up (albeit with bumps and bruises). We are fortunate that God is patient, compassionate, and forgiving, and that he has a sense of humor. Could Jesus have endured the disciples, or God the church, were it otherwise?

God chose to save us through Jesus, so it would seem wise, healthy, and even holy to quit trying to save ourselves through autonomous efforts. We are asked to participate in, not assume responsibility for, the salvation of ourselves and the world through grace (cf. Col 1:24). Our role in salvation history remains free, authentic, and dignified, but ancillary. We are made in God's image and likeness to represent and reflect him through dominion (stewardship), life giving (creative and pro-creative love), and justice (right relationships), but we are ultimately limited and dependent creatures, formed from the soil and destined to return there (cf. Gn 2:7, 3:19). Let us keep our responsible but interdependent role in mind as we endeavor to manage our energies, gifts, and responsibilities for God's glory and our own legitimate good pleasure.

Reflection Exercises

What role and priority in my life do I give prayer?

Are there any practices, commitments, or attitude adjustments I can undertake that would support my efforts to pray and live prayerfully? How could I better integrate prayer with integrity of living and working?

What are my beliefs regarding God's providence and initiative in human affairs? Is he active and trustworthy, or does he leave us completely to our own efforts?

How have I experienced God's providence and initiative in my life?

Reflections, Applications, and Little Victories

3

Perspective and Poise

Perspective and poise are aspects of self-possession. They constitute the attitudes and viewpoints from which we interpret life, and the degree of self-control with which we respond to events. In this chapter, we explore the role they assume in our quest for personal and professional effectiveness.

Perspective

We will not be able to channel our energies, abilities, emotions, and opportunities in a constructive manner without a healthy perspective. Our outlook on life is the underlying criterion we use for interpreting and responding to events. This has great bearing on our emotions and attitudes. Because perspective is intertwined with personal values and beliefs, individuals understand and develop their perspective on life within the context of their personal belief system. Perspective is the foundation upon which all Personal Energy Management efforts are built. It is prudent to consider periodically to what degree we are living and working in harmony with our outlook on life. Internal and external factors can influence us positively or negatively, and either contribute to our mission or throw us off course.

Reality is both the objective and subjective criterion for evaluating our perspective. Perspective is essentially a quest for truth and understanding. It consists of seeing things in their proper dimensions and helps us keep our balance by viewing everything in context. This enables us to approach life as a unified whole, rather than as a series of unrelated events and situations. Perspective is the filter through which we understand and discern circumstances.

If we develop a long-term perspective, we will be better able to absorb the setbacks we experience. It can serve as a buffer against extreme mood swings and daily disappointments and frustrations. By keeping the broad picture before us, we can make better judgments as to how to exert and direct our energies and emotions. A wise spiritual director once commented to me: "Many of our frustrations and anxieties remain with us because we lose sight of the long term. Most situations work out in the long run, if only we are patient and compliant." The fullness and underlying truth in situations grows in clarity with time.

Any personal growth journey must begin at, and continually return to, the intersection of the heart and the mind. We must take a long look at how we view the world and ourselves, not to judge or criticize, but to understand. The more we are at peace with ourselves and our understanding of the world, the more poised we will be in action. Let us now reflect upon one of the first fruits of a healthy perspective: poise.

Poise: Progeny of Perspective

Few virtues are more challenging and elusive than poise, or self-control. Poise requires a substantial degree of self-discipline and confidence; it implies that we relate to people and events in a calm, purposeful manner. How difficult it is to maintain our poise when others have lost theirs, and our world seems to be crashing in around us!

I resist defining *poise* because there are so many ways it can manifest itself. In modern jargon, poise is keeping cool. Poise is directing and channeling our emotions and response reflexes rather than letting them control us. It brings our instinctive reactions and impulses into dialogue with our rationality and morality, and gives practical, immediate expression to self-direction and self-control. Individuals who control themselves, especially their tongues, have mastered their most dangerous enemy. How do we develop such control?

Silence: The Context of Composure

The first and most basic building block and sustainer of perspective and poise is a personal commitment to and cultivation of silence. We will be unable to maintain any type of perspective over the long haul without a healthy experience of silence. Chronic noise promotes confusion, while silence fosters calm.

There are many ways in which we can cultivate silence. When presenting workshops on wellness and stress transformation to both Christian and secular audiences, I recommend at least three minutes of quiet time twice a day, stressing that we are to be patient with ourselves on days when we fail to do this. This commitment is not overwhelming, and does not evoke guilt or scrupulosity. It serves as a good starting point and a healthy challenge that fosters self-discipline and, usually, a desire for more quiet time with God, nature, ourselves, or others.

Nature provides many settings of natural quiet and pleasant noise that are conducive to relaxation, reflection, and contemplation (that is, simply being with life and its creator). The ocean, woods, mountains, streams, and wildlife can provide us with a soothing backdrop for reflection. One therapeutic and stimulating aspect of nature is that of flowing water, whether in the form of a river, babbling brook, or waterfall. The therapeutic qualities of flowing water have been known to the oriental world since ancient times. Oriental monarchs often make provision for flowing water or waterfalls in their gardens. We can also refer to the second creation narrative in Genesis, which includes a geographical detail concerning the source of the four great rivers of the ancient world, and also describes the watering of the garden in Eden (cf. Gn 2:10–14). The energy, nutrients, and aesthetic beauty of water are vital to life and to the healthy cultivation of silence and composure.

Our hectic lifestyles and schedules present us with many decisions on a daily basis. How can we approach these decisions from a position of strength unless we have a reservoir of silence from which we can reflect and respond? *It is important for us to carve out a few moments or minutes, perhaps several times a day, to relax, be still, and listen.* Our senses take in many conflicting stimuli throughout the day, and these distractions can drown out the quiet voice that springs to us from the heart. Daily periods of silence joined with an open heart enable us to hear the still, small voice of intuition, reason, and conscience that reverberates within us. How can we listen to others if we refuse to listen to ourselves?

Letting Go of the Little Things

How easy it is to let little things get the best of us: the rude driver, the grumpy customer or salesperson, the moody boss, the inconsiderate friend, and just plain old bad timing—for example, being held up by a crossing train for ten minutes when you are in a hurry. The big things we seem to handle, while the little things drive us crazy.

Poise and perspective work together to help us calm ourselves amid life's harrowing aggravations. What good does it do to get exasperated over something that has no significant long-term effects, and that is only a temporary annoyance? We cannot eliminate or become immune to life's irritations or "positive-think" them away, but we can put them in perspective and see them for what they are: annoying pebbles in our shoes. They may irritate us temporarily, but they need not incite us to throw away our shoe to rid ourselves of the pebble. By using perspective to keep the big picture of life in view, and developing the poise necessary for responding to immediate situations in a rational and composed manner, we can either remove or endure these pebbles. They no longer thwart us from our goal, or impede us from receiving all that each moment and day offers us.

The Four Basic Human Relationships

There are many books on healthy self-love and human relationships from both secular humanist and Christian perspectives. Although they are helpful, none can match the succinct and incisive wisdom and existential truths of the inspired Word of God. Scripture often cuts through complicated concepts and theories with deep and direct statements concerning humanity's various relationships.

The four basic human relationships—with ourselves, God, others, and the natural and material world—provide a framework for study and reflection on Scripture. Keeping these relationships in mind when we read the Bible, we can ask ourselves the following question: What truths about healthy or unhealthy relationships does this passage contain, and how might God be calling me to apply these insights to my life?

Sources of Our Images of Self, God, Others, and the Natural and Material World

The following relationships and environments help shape our perspective on life. Each relationship or environment contains both positive and negative influences on how we view the Four Basic Relationships. As these factors evolve over time we may modify our judgment on the efficacy of our Four Basic Relationships, as well as the environments in which those relationships are defined and developed.

1. Family education

2. Formal education
   a. secular
   b. religious

3. Cultural influence

4. Peer group influence

5. Personal experiences

Inner Healing Exercise*

The above influences can be to varying degrees positive or negative. When they reinforce an image of a personal, involved, caring God, they foster development of a healthy relationship with God. Distorted perspectives on the Four Basic Relationships affect everyone, and in turn are perpetuated by all. We receive and transmit such negative images even (and sometimes especially) to those we love.

Ask Jesus to heal the pain in your life that colors your perception of the Four Basic Relationships. If you are able, pray for the grace to forgive those who have contributed to the unhealthy perspective that you operate out of. When you ask, believe that you will be healed. Petition God if you lack trust (cf. Mk 9:14–29). Pray for the gift of acceptance and understanding concerning the nature and timing of healing that you receive. Permit God the same freedom he extends to us.

The intense nature of this exercise makes it appropriate primarily for retreatants, Christian support groups, and individuals with access to a spiritual director, pastoral counselor, or therapist.

Inspiration to Self-Abandonment from Saint Ignatius

"Take, Lord, and receive all my liberty, my memory, my understanding, and all my will—all that I have and possess. You, Lord, have given all that to me. I now give it back to you, O Lord. All of it is yours. Dispose of it according to your will. Give me love of yourself along with your grace, for that is enough for me" (taken from "Contemplation to Attain Love," in George Ganss, S.J., trans., *The Spiritual Exercises of Saint Ignatius*).

Conclusion

When engaging in introspection, it is most important to emphasize patience, the mercy of God, and self-forgiveness. Avoid rash, harsh self-indictments. In areas where authentic guilt and sin play a part, avoid being a "Lone Ranger." Ask God for forgiveness, accept it, reconcile with your brother or sister (if necessary), the church (if necessary), and rejoice at the new possibilities. Many people lack the courage and integrity to confront their naked selves. If you make the decision to try to be objective and honest, you open yourself up to God's providence and mercy. Such risk taking is a wonderful form of cooperation with the Spirit, and will yield abundant fruits in God's time and way.

Our personal perspective has the greatest influence over our attitudes and behaviors. Poise flows from perspective, rationality, and self-control, and helps us remain calm while those around us run helter-skelter and spin their wheels. It is a virtue that grows with patience and maturity. While it is important to understand the roots of our vision, what is most important is the lifelong reformulation, deepening, and actualization of that vision. In the next chapter, we examine the catalyst of the Personal Energy Management process: personal or collective purpose.

Reflection Exercises

How would I describe my outlook on life? Does it empower or inhibit me? How do I view myself, others, God and religion, nature, and the material world?

How does my perspective manifest itself in daily life? In how I treat others? In my attitude toward myself, including the way I talk to myself internally? Do I exhibit respect for myself and others? Do I live and work in harmony with my perspective?

How do I view and respond to the environment, other living creatures, and material possessions? Do I see them as something to be responsibly and creatively enjoyed, or as items to be utilized for functional reasons and temporary pleasures?

What adjectives, nouns, or verbs would characterize my perspective or attitudes toward the Four Basic Relationships?

Self	God	Others	Natural and Material World

Are there situations, personalities, or behaviors that induce me to lose my poise?

What corrective measures or attitudinal changes would help me display greater self-control?

Reflections, Applications, and Little Victories

4

Purpose: Catalyst of Individual and Collective Effectiveness

M otivational speakers and writers frequently speak of the concept of human potential without defining it. This ambiguity is attributable to the fact that potential is a function of purpose. The way we define and work toward our potential will depend on the ends to which we intend to use our capabilities and resources. Each of us possesses a tremendous amount of both positive and negative potential.

The importance of *purpose*, or personal meaning, in the human development process is underscored brilliantly in the psychological school known as *logotherapy*. Founded by Viktor Frankl and inspired by his grim but enlightening experience in the Nazi concentration camp at Auschwitz (see his book *Man's Search for Meaning*), logotherapy has brought to the psychotherapeutic world a convincing testimony of the role of personal meaning in both health and disease. Sustained motivation and effectiveness is impossible without a core of personal meaning to help us persevere through difficult times.

In the context of Personal Energy Management, logotherapy is a reminder that our quest for personal effectiveness must be founded on and energized by integrity, that is, faithfulness to core values and beliefs. Both organizations and individuals must have a charter, whether specified or implicit, to provide criteria for determining the success or failure of their efforts and mission.

Purpose is communicated in the organizational world through mission statements that articulate shared values and goals. Individuals need a sense of mission or purpose to help them stay on course amid the waves of distractions and enticing side alleys that arise on a daily basis. Because self-knowledge is the foundation of self-motivation, let us discuss the purpose and structure of a personal mission statement, while providing an example and an exercise for articulating our own.

Statement of Mission or Vocation

A *mission statement* is a concise, heartfelt statement of our perceived purpose and calling in life. It is the fundamental criteria by which we evaluate our response to life and work situations. A mission statement is based on our values, beliefs, and hopes. It should be relatively brief, ranging from a sentence to a paragraph or two. We are the sole judge of its efficacy. Recalling our mission statement periodically can help us recenter ourselves on our fundamental mission. We know how easy it is to lose sight of our central path and direction in life. As our life vision and sense of purpose or vocation evolves, we can revise and update our mission statement.

The following is a sample statement of mission or vocation:

I wish to be faithful to my beliefs and values, to myself and those I love, and to do my best in every situation. I try to enjoy, treasure, and accept life with a peaceful, humble, and joyful spirit. I strive to live by the Golden Rule, and to be a person of understanding and compassion.

Ultimately, we serve someone or something. Whether it is ourselves, others, God, a cause, or a goal, we eventually reveal our loyalties. Our actions can advance or detract from our purpose. Once we identify our purpose, and begin to build our developmental efforts around it, we will have a foundation capable of sustaining us through the inevitable ups and downs of life. This sense of purpose, mission, vocation, or meaning is the lens through which we view and discern the integrity and effectiveness of our efforts.

Reflection Exercises

As preparation for composing a personal mission statement, try to articulate what you feel is your underlying purpose or goal(s) in life. What inspires, reassures, and motivates you at home and at work? What gives meaning to your life and toil?

Cite examples where a sense of purpose has helped you grow, cope, or achieve.

What are your reasons for working in your current job or career? In the context of the practical constraints and circumstances in your life, are these reasons acceptable?

Do you affirm yourself for living and working with integrity, that is, attempting to be faithful to your core beliefs and values? What words, actions, or practices do you use to affirm yourself?

When you suffer or experience disappointment because of your devotion to a person, principle, or cause, do you make an attempt to comfort yourself in some way? How?

Conversely, when your commitment and fidelity bears fruit, do you make the time and effort to acknowledge and celebrate the good news or experience?

Statement of Mission or Vocation: Articulate in heartfelt language your conception of your mission in life both personally and professionally. Write a statement or paragraph that describes your personal standard of integrity and fidelity.

Reflections, Applications, and Little Victories

5

Self-Knowledge and Discernment

I t is difficult to imagine how we will be able to maximize our potential if we are uncertain about our capabilities, aptitudes, and life direction. Personal growth is founded on a truthful self-understanding. Paralleling the many extensive and generally expensive tests and programs designed to improve self-knowledge are several practical and manageable exercises that we explore in this chapter: strengths and weaknesses inventory, goal definition, and values assessment. These basic, time-proven exercises build on our sense of purpose, mission, or vocation, and are ideal for assessing our situation and direction both personally and professionally. Our first activity is to assess our resources and limitations. Before we embark upon any mission or encounter we must determine that we have the necessary or potential resources and capabilities.

Strengths and Weaknesses Inventory

Human beings possess a complex plethora of strengths and weaknesses in various stages of development. Confusion and self-doubt may result from the resistance or lack of affirmation, support, or cooperation we receive from others as we try to develop our gifts and operate within our limitations. Sometimes we fail to recognize personal gifts and attributes due to the lack of encouragement or feedback supplied by others, be they family, friends, or peers. A good rule of thumb, assuming we are not deluding ourselves, is to trust our deepest gut feelings, especially if they are accompanied by humility, accurate information, and objectivity. Despite our culture's preference for winning and being number one, we do not have to be the best at whatever we do, as long as we give our best.

Patience is an essential component of self-development. We do not discover and develop our personal vocation, gifts, and boundaries overnight. Virtues in one environment or culture might be considered detriments in another. For example, a gifted communicator with a pleasing personality may thrive as a teacher, but drown in a sea of figures and formality when in an accounting position. Many people with outstanding talents have met consistent rejection before finding a person or environment that recognizes their capabilities. Americans have been conditioned by culture and advertising to desire risk-free, painless, guaranteed results, rather than pursue values-centered goals that require sacrifice and hard work. The crucial point pertaining to strengths and weaknesses is not to place all our faith in first impressions or experiences, or in the opinions of others. Our gifts and limitations are in various stages of development, with some of the seeds needing only cultivation, timing, and the right soil.

Personal Attributes Assessment

The rating system of this assessment is left to your creative discretion. You may choose scales of 1 to 10, poor to excellent, *A* to *F,* and so on, or you may write prose assessment statements next to each attribute. The objective is simply to identify and evaluate your gifts. Thoroughness and honesty are the major ingredients of a successful self-inventory. Be as brief or as descriptive as necessary. For example, if you know you possess a mediocre singing voice, and have no desire to improve it, state your thoughts briefly and move on. Spend more time on attributes you are either unsure about or would like to develop.

1. Next to each attribute in the following list, rate or discuss the measure in which you believe you possess it.

2. Add any qualities that apply to you and are missing. Do not be modest.

3. Double-check your analysis. Sometimes first impressions are incomplete and need to be critically evaluated.

4. At your discretion, review your assessment with a trusted confidant or mentor and elicit feedback. If the response is uniformly negative or positive, beware.

Positive Qualities

enthusiasm

honesty

sincerity

persistence

lightheartedness

attention to detail

patience

efficiency

concentration (on a task or object)

presence (to a person or people)

awareness

balance, moderation, temperance

concentric perspective (ability to see parts in relation to the whole) self-control, self-discipline

ingenuity, creativity

trust or faith

hope

love

detachment

self-confidence

humility

loyalty

obedience

showmanship

thriftiness

flexibility, spontaneity

adaptability, resilience

decisiveness

effective communicator (clear and concise)

purposefulness

manual dexterity

athletic ability

pleasing personality

sense of humor

skilled judge of character

leadership skills

tolerance

cooperativeness

industriousness

adventurousness

poise, composure

Weaknesses and Limitations Assessment

The rating system of this assessment is left to your creative discretion. You may use scales of 1 to 10 or homemade evaluation systems (for example: relevant, unsure, irrelevant; or some, much, none), or you may write prose assessment statements next to each shortcoming. The objective is simply to identify and acknowledge your limitations. This exercise not only provides a healthy dose of self-knowledge and humility, but it also removes the aura of mystery that so often surrounds our hidden faults and weaknesses. You can more easily discover your true strengths when you have accepted your true weaknesses. Prideful shame and insecurity does no one any good.

1. Next to each shortcoming in the following list, rate or discuss the measure in which you believe you possess it. Be sure to recognize gray areas, and spend some time in reflection on these.

2. How are you going to neutralize your major weaknesses? Remember, we are not interested in seeking perfection, but in making the best of the situation.

3. At your discretion, review your assessment with a trusted confidant or mentor and elicit feedback.

Shortcomings

procrastination

narcissism

"something for nothing" mentality

critical assessment of others

legalism, literalism

scrupulosity

incompetence

indecisiveness, vacillation

excessive pride, arrogance

complacency

indifference

fatalism

irresponsibility

quitter mentality

manipulativeness

oppressiveness

rigidity

self-centeredness

aversion to criticism, hypersensitivity

fearfulness

worrisomeness

indiscriminate preference for uniformity and conformity

extreme stubbornness

Goal Definition

The *P* parameters discussed in this book flow from the fundamental goals and mission to which we wish to be faithful. Unlike many personal development authors, I do not place inordinate emphasis on goals. They are more important as guidelines than as ends in themselves. We should observe a certain moderation and prudence in our pursuit of goals. Achievement of goals should be accompanied by respect for the integrity of the process and our efforts. Sometimes the ability to achieve our goals, especially within a given time frame, is subject to factors beyond our control. Therefore, it is important to keep our goals in perspective and to value the process as much as the end results.

Attributes of Healthy Goals

We can define in one sentence the primary prerequisites of goal definition: We should strive to set goals that are manageable, divisible (into incremental steps or parts), meaningful (reasonably compatible with our hopes, values, beliefs, and dreams), measurable, dynamic (amenable to change and development), economical and efficient (all things being equal, why not take the straightest path to our destination?), and specific and precise (ambiguity provides a ready-made excuse for failure, getting sidetracked, or quitting).

Positive Goal Attributes

1. Manageable

2. Divisible, susceptible to miniaturization

3. Meaningful

4. Measurable

5. Dynamic

6. Economical and efficient

7. Specific and precise: clarity is charity

Goal Definition Checklist

1. Expect to modify your original goals and expectations to suit changing perceptions and circumstances.
   a. The more difficult the process, the more likely the need for revision.
   b. Be wary of completely dispensing with your original goal based on early returns. Give the process time.

2. Achievement of a secondary goal can be a blessing in disguise.
   a. Utilize secondary goals as an emotional cushion during rough times. Worst-case scenarios and "plan Bs" prepare us for failed expectations. They can inspire us to work even when the main goal seems remote. Such alternate courses enable us to respond to changing circumstances and take advantage of opportunities that arise.

3. Trust your intuitive, gut-level feelings and experiences when making judgments.

4. Avoid incessant second-guessing at all costs.
   a. Evaluate the situation, assimilate the facts and educational portion, make any necessary decisions, then move on. Keep mental anguish to a minimum. Save it for serious problems (for example: death, separation, disability, and so on).

5. Be selective in choosing your advisers.
   a. Do not assume that your advisers are always correct, especially in areas foreign to their expertise.

Expectations: Goal Complement or Detriment?

1. Our internal expectations must be consistent with our stated goal.

2. Vague expectations are an invitation to mediocrity.

3. Excessively low or high expectations will detract from the achievement process by stimulating underachievement or discouragement.

Goal Definition Exercises

Mindful of guidelines presented in this section, formulate your goal(s).

Write a concise and persuasive paragraph or two justifying your goal(s) in light of the principles and attributes delineated above.

Review your responses to the strengths and weaknesses inventory, and the forthcoming values assessment. Which strengths, weaknesses, and values are particularly relevant to your short-term and long-term goals? Discuss how you will utilize your attributes and values in working toward your goals.

Values Clarification

Because of the intense and widespread way in which societal values are thrust into our home and work environments, it is essential that we monitor the degree to which we are living and working in faithfulness to our values. *Values* are the core beliefs and principles that influence our thoughts, emotions, and actions. They are the guts and internal mobilizer that undergirds our activities, skills, and decisions. Perhaps even more so than beliefs or concepts, values are the impetus to change and conversion. Values are the incarnation of beliefs, the fuel of skills, and the backbone of behavior.

There are many helpful values clarification tests and workshops available, which we would do well to consult during periods of discernment and transition. My understanding of values is derived largely from the creative and practical insights of Dr. Brian P. Hall, especially as reflected in his influential book, *The Genesis Effect*. As Dr. Hall eloquently articulates, values are the primary stimulants to personal, relational, and organizational transformation. The general categories I use in the following values assessment exercise are drawn from Dr. Hall's work, which also takes the form of detailed, scientific values clarification and discernment tools.

Complementing the scientific and empirical instruments mentioned above are simpler, more practical ways of assessing whether or not we are developing our strengths, weaknesses, and values, and actualizing them in daily life and work situations. The following values assessment exercise is designed to help us clarify the things we value most in life. It is not a scientific or psychological tool, but a practical exercise designed to prime our thoughts and help us focus on areas in our lives that demand our attention and energy.

Values Assessment

1. Next to each value in the following sample list, describe briefly its importance to you. If it is unimportant, you may simply write (N/A) and move on. Spend the

majority of the time on those values that hold importance for you.

2. After completing the above evaluation, make a list of
the values that hold the greatest importance for you.
(Use the clarification prompters below to aid you in
making your list.) You can validate your list by observing your everyday thought and behavior patterns.
They should not contradict your values list. If the values are not reflected in your everyday living, you may
need to clarify your values further. Then, if necessary,
revise your values list.

*Answer based on who you are now, rather than who
you wish to be. If you are unhappy with your current
values system, this exercise can be the first step in
reconstructing it.*

Clarification Prompters

When you need to make an important decision, what
are the most compelling considerations?

If someone were to try to influence or persuade you on
a matter, what issues or areas of interest would they
appeal to?

What values epitomize the people with whom you have
your most frequent conflicts?

What types of people do you find yourself most comfortable with in regard to emotionally intimate relationships? (We gravitate toward those with whom we
share core values.)

The values you project for yourself should reveal
themselves in practical circumstances. Unless they are
evidenced in your lifestyle and behavior, their authen-
ticity is questionable.

3. Discuss the origins of your values system. What messages did you hear as a child? Discuss your recollec-
tions and feelings in detail.

4. (Optional) Review your hierarchy with a trustworthy friend, mentor, or confidant, and elicit feedback. Select someone who is open, interested, and nonjudgmental.

Sample Values Grouped by Category

Safety and Survival

dwelling (for example: house, land, apartment)

financial security

emotional security and well-being, peace of mind

physical security, safety

adventure (risk taking)

Relational

family

marriage

friendships

social status, prestige

social justice, concern for human dignity

belonging (acceptance by others)

community

social acceptance, compliance with social and institutional standards

interpersonal harmony, avoidance of conflict

Vocational

peer respect, recognition, professional image

originality, creativity

responsibility, autonomy

education, career advancement, potential realization

Universal

health, physical fitness

physical appearance

independence, autonomy

tradition, continuity

competence, efficiency

personal development, potential realization

personal integrity

authority

religion, meaning

sense of duty or responsibility, accountability

sensate pleasure

technological progress

politics, power

education, knowledge, understanding, wisdom

Leisure

> aesthetic interests and activities (for example: art, music, history)
>
> practical knowledge and hands-on activities
>
> silence, reflection space
>
> personal remembrance or memories, nostalgia
>
> hobbies in general, pastimes (for example: sports)
>
> nature

Conclusion

We have briefly reviewed the practical importance of such fundamental tools as mission statements, goal setting, strength and weakness inventories, and values assessment exercises. There is a subtle danger in taking these fundamentals for granted and presuming that our current direction and behavior is in harmony with our true selves and the common good. The concluding *P* principles, perseverance and prudence, help actualize and develop this self-knowledge through experience, understanding, and endurance.

Reflections, Applications, and Little Victories

6

Perseverance and Prudence: The Guts and Stabilizer of Success

One of the crucial elements of our human values approach is that of keeping our eyes focused on long-term objectives and results. No matter how hard we work at an objective, in the short term there will be a prevailing element of external variables, providence, and timing that will influence the outcome. In the long term, this uncontrollable element remains but is diminished due to the law of averages and the increased effect and influence of our efforts. In order to experience the fruit of our labor, we must work through short-term ups and downs.

There is truth in the adage that nothing good comes easily. This is why perseverance is so important. We must be willing to keep going even when all seems lost. We must quit only when it becomes apparent that is the better choice. Perseverance has a contagious effect. Those around us see it, and are often inspired by it. Actions speak louder than words.

Perseverance energizes us because it keeps us from getting bogged down in the temporary failures that we experience. It affects and empowers us on a subconscious level as well. We send a message to our whole selves when we persist: We are not going to be denied. We may not succeed as we envisioned or prefer, but it will not be for lack of trying.

Persist or Desist

Not infrequently during the growth and achievement process does the question of discernment arise: When is enough enough? At what point do I retool and go in a different direction? When does persistence in interactions with others become pushiness? When is persistence primarily fueled by ego-related stubbornness rather than detached (in the spiritual sense of moderate, rather than inordinate, attachment) commitment to a worthwhile cause?

There is no easy solution for confronting this perplexing issue. Any worthwhile endeavor will have its discouraging periods. There will be times when we will wonder whether it is all worth it. Sometimes we will need to take time out, regroup, and rethink our strategy. A balanced integration of reflection, prayer, counsel, and analysis can help us come to a responsible decision. In the end, we must go with what we feel at our deepest level, and what we believe to be right. We may have to confront the persist, desist, or tread water question a number of times along our journey. Each situation has dynamics that reveal whether it is better to err on the side of persistence or prudence. There are opportunity costs and risks associated with each. Prudence helps us answer these questions through analysis, intuition, and judgment.

Prudence

Dictionaries define *prudence* as wisdom in practical matters. What this means, and how it applies to specific situations, has both an objective and subjective element. There are many helpful guidelines and principles we can offer for specific circumstances, but there is always an element of discretion that can be determined only by the people involved.

Prudence is the art of integrating general, practical wisdom with personal intuition and discernment. It is the skill of making reasonable and intuitive choices in life and work situations. Prudence is discretion, caution, and judgment born of education, formation, and experience.

In a concise book such as ours, which integrates spirituality and personal development the best directives and suggestions we can offer come from the Scriptures. Concluding this chapter are a selection of proverbs from Hebrew wisdom literature that provide good counsel for common situations. They are only the tip of the iceberg; refer to your Bible for amplification and context.

Prudence: The Harmonizing and Stabilizing Value

Personal Energy Management is fundamentally the art of prudence. It is difficult to offer specific directives to generic issues and situations because most circumstances contain variables that transcend generalities and require particular attention and discernment. For example, how should we present ourselves and interact on the telephone? Which activities take priority? How can we outmaneuver our procrastination tendencies? Where is the line between excellence and obsession?

Prudence is a whole-person virtue because it confronts the central, practical, and frequently ambiguous questions of life and work. Prudence is the process of bringing our rational, emotional, moral, spiritual, creative, and intuitive faculties together for the purpose of deciding and acting in a wise manner. We know how easy it is to let any of the above faculties dominate our decision-making and responding processes, and create an imbalance. Knowing how to balance and integrate these dimensions is a skill and virtue we develop with the aid of family, friends, teachers, educational resources, prayers, and perhaps most of all, experience. We can come to our best understanding of prudence by reflecting on specific life and work experiences and dilemmas. What decisions and actions seemed wise, which responses missed the mark?

The more deeply we reflect upon prudence, the more apparent our need for the counsel and support of others becomes. Prudence is both an individual and communal challenge, with far more questions and lessons than easy answers. Why not learn from and build upon the insights and experiences of others? We cannot absorb the whole range of practical wisdom in our lifetime, and it is tiresome and inefficient to reinvent the wheel with each new challenge and endeavor. This brings us to the most practical and spiritual reason for concluding the chapter with wisdom proverbs. Who better to counsel us in our journey than the Holy Spirit?

Perseverance, Purpose, and Prudence

Perseverance, purpose, and prudence go hand in hand in the process of personal effectiveness. Unbridled, imprudent perseverance can lead us into an obsessive and inefficient pursuit of our goals. The virtue of endurance can easily gravitate toward the vice of obstinacy. Prudence enables us to make responsible and enlightened decisions on gray matters and pivotal (and sometimes painful) issues. Perseverance without purpose yields diffuse energy and ambiguous results. Purpose is the overall direction and values system to which we wish to be faithful. It provides us with an idea or image of where we are going, and what we wish to accomplish.

Imprudent perseverance complicates and aggravates situations. Purposeless perseverance reduces the potency and clarity of our efforts. In both cases, we undermine and weaken the integrity and efficacy of our efforts. Self-direction is the modern term for the integration of purpose, self-understanding, and healthy autonomy. Goals are specific manifestations and applications of self-direction in light of situation and circumstance. Goals are realized through the actualization of a purposeful charter of activities and direction of energy—in other words, a daily and short-term modus operandi and game plan. In the next chapter, which begins the Personal Energy Management Practices section, we explore the role of priorities in the process of realizing our goals and dreams, and channeling our energies, resources, and abilities in an effective manner.

Reflection Exercises

What areas in my life or work require me to persevere beyond my comfort level? Does this help me grow as a person and strengthen me, or does it weaken and demoralize me? Is my perseverance prudent and virtuous or excessive and unhealthy?

How would I define prudence, and what role does it play in my life and work? Am I conscious of the importance of thinking, acting, and communicating prudently in both personal and professional situations?

Are there situations, attitudes, behaviors, or relationships in my personal life in which I need more prudence? Cite relevant past or present experiences that have brought this to your attention.

Are there situations, attitudes, behaviors, or relationships in my professional life in which I need more prudence? Cite relevant past or present experiences that have brought this to your attention.

Proverbs from Proverbs

1:7   "The fear of the LORD is the beginning of knowledge; wisdom and instruction fools despise."

3:27   "Refuse no one the good on which he has a claim when it is in your power to do it for him."

11:14   "For lack of guidance a people falls; security lies in many counselors."

12:1   "He who loves correction loves knowledge, but he who hates reproof is stupid."

12:23   "A shrewd man conceals his knowledge, but the hearts of fools gush forth folly."

12:25   "Anxiety in a man's heart depresses it, but a kindly word makes it glad."

13:11   "Wealth quickly gotten dwindles away, but amassed little by little, it grows."

13:20   "Walk with wise men and you will become wise, but the companion of fools will fare badly."

14:15–16 "The simpleton believes everything, but the shrewd man measures his steps. The wise man is cautious and shuns evil; the fool is reckless and sure of himself."

14:29–30 "The patient man shows much good sense, but the quick-tempered man displays folly at its height. A tranquil mind gives life to the body, but jealousy rots the bones."

15:4   "A soothing tongue is a tree of life, but a perverse one crushes the spirit."

15:13   "A glad heart lights up the face, but by mental anguish the spirit is broken."

15:15–17 "Every day is miserable for the depressed, but a lighthearted man has a continual feast. Better a little with fear of the LORD than a great fortune with anxiety. Better a dish of herbs where love is than a fatted ox and hatred with it."

15:27   "He who is greedy of gain brings ruin on his own house, but he who hates bribes will live."

16:8–9   "Better a little with virtue, than a large income with injustice. In his mind a man plans his course, but the LORD directs his steps."

17:9	"He who covers up a misdeed fosters friendship, but he who gossips about it separates friends."
17:10	"A single reprimand does more for a man of intelligence than a hundred lashes for a fool."
17:22	"A joyful heart is the health of the body, but a depressed spirit dries up the bones."
17:27	"He who spares his word is truly wise, and he who is chary of speech is a man of intelligence."
17:28	"Even a fool, if he keeps silent, is considered wise; if he closes his lips, intelligent."
18:21	"Death and life are in the power of the tongue; those who make it a friend shall eat its fruit."
19:2	"Without knowledge even zeal is not good; and he who acts hastily, blunders."
19:11	"It is good sense in a man to be slow to anger, and it is his glory to overlook an offense."
20:14	"'Bad, bad!' says the buyer; but once he has gone his way, he boasts."
24:16–18	"For the just man falls seven times and rises again, but the wicked stumble to ruin. Rejoice not when your enemy falls, and when he stumbles, let not your heart exult, Lest the LORD see it, be displeased with you, and withdraw his wrath from your enemy."
24:23	"These are also sayings of the wise: To show partiality in judgment is not good."
25:9–11	"Discuss your case with your neighbor, but another man's secret do not disclose; Lest, hearing it, he reproach you, and your ill repute cease not. Like golden apples in silver settings are words spoken at the proper time."
25:15	"By patience is a ruler persuaded, and a soft tongue will break a bone."
25:28	"Like an open city with no defenses is the man with no check on his feelings."
28:23	"He who rebukes a man gets more thanks in the end than one with a flattering tongue."
29:11	"The fool gives vent to all his anger; but by biding his time, the wise man calms it."

Reflections, Applications, and Little Victories

Personal Energy Management *P* Parameters Review and Preview

Part one contains the principles and foundations of Personal Energy Management. In part two we explore practical applications and actualization of these concepts. Keep in mind that these principles, practices, and the possibilities and pitfalls discussed in part three are relevant to both personal and professional situations. They can help us balance and integrate work and home in a more healthy and holy fashion.

Important Reminder:
The Reflections, Applications, and Little Victories page that concludes each chapter can be used to record our insights on work and home issues as well as other applications, feelings, questions, and experiences. Because the journey is part of the destination, we cannot expect to achieve complete understanding and competence on any issue. The reflection space provided with each chapter can serve as a journal in which we record our struggles, doubts, pains, and insecurities, as well as our hopes and triumphs.

Review

Principles
Philosophy
Prayer and Providence
Perspective and Poise
Purpose
Self-Knowledge and Discernment
Perseverance and Prudence

Preview

Practices
Priorities

Personal and Professional Rhythm: Pace, Patience, and Patterns
Presence to the Present
Persuasion
Desk, File, and Phone Management

Possibilities and Pitfalls
Procrastination
Perfectionism
Punctuality
Rediscovering Leisure

Part Two

Personal Energy Management Applications
The *P* Practices

1

The *ABC*s of Prioritizing

*P**rioritizing** is the practice of ordering our activities in such
a way that we do the right thing at the right time. Timing is
as important as content. We prioritize in recognition of the
trade-offs and opportunity costs that exist in all facets of life:
doing one thing at a certain time restricts us from doing something else. The goal is to direct our efforts toward spending our
time and energy in the most fruitful way and at the appropriate
time. Both importance (content) and urgency (timing) must be
weighed, with importance being the ultimate tiebreaker.

In previous chapters we developed a foundation for prioritizing in the form of values, goals, capabilities, and mission. In this
chapter, we examine the mechanics and concepts of prioritizing
as they build upon this foundation. Our objective in prioritizing
complements that of growing in self-knowledge: We want to put
our efforts, energies, and capabilities to maximum use.

Knowing Our *ABC*s

Most systems for prioritizing rank activities within three categories. Although the terminology used to describe these categories may be different, the concepts are generally the same.
We will use the *ABC* nomenclature because it is the simplest.

To help us prioritize, we can rank on paper all activities
according to their relative importance and urgency. Because prioritizing is an inexact science based on imperfect information,

we must give up any expectations of certitude and perfection. Instead, we should learn to make decisions and actualize them in a confident and competent manner. The concepts of materiality (that is, energy should be expended in accordance with the subject's relative importance) and simplicity can help us avoid making prioritizing a project in itself. We must always remember this question: Which tasks are most important, and when are they done optimally?

Our classification system is as follows: *A* priorities are must dos, *B* priorities are preferably dos, and *C* priorities are maybe dos. These can change with new information and time. For example, preparing an income tax return is a *C* priority in January both because the return is not due for a while and because we may not have all the financial and tax information we need. However, if we know we will be extremely busy in March and April, we might give serious thought to beginning our preparations in January. In the case of a tax return, the consequences of tardiness are severe, so our task will rank fairly high in importance, and progressively higher in urgency.

As our example demonstrates, prioritizing involves a comprehensive planning process that takes into account our short-, intermediate-, and long-term needs and objectives. The more we prioritize, the more mistakes we will become aware of, and hopefully learn from. When we fail to prioritize, we may not be immediately aware of the opportunity costs of not ordering our activities in an effective manner. Prioritizing is not a solution to the ambiguities of decision making, but a way of making informed and sincere choices.

To avoid confusion, it is helpful to compile separate lists of priorities based on the *ABC* categories. There may be some movement between these lists as new information and circumstances evolve. Housecleaning moves from a *C* to an *A* priority when the in-laws surprise you with an announcement of their impending arrival. New clothes rise in priority when a significant social or business event comes onto the horizon. Purchasing a household item declines in priority upon news of a household member's layoff.

Once we complete a task, it is encouraging to cross the item from our list and acknowledge our progression. It is a good idea to reward ourselves periodically for good work; we may wait a long time for others to recognize our efforts. There are little bonuses we can give ourselves for a job well done. This is especially true when the major fruits of our labor are in doubt, or loom solely as long-term rewards. It is too easy to get depressed or find our morale slipping when we are working on an important task replete with difficulties and with no end in sight. The ideal is to interject personal and creative rewards into the prioritizing process, and thereby enhance our ability to persevere and work effectively.

An important guideline is to define priorities in a relaxed atmosphere. It is difficult to think straight when rushed or under pressure. Setting priorities for home or work on the day or evening before ensures that we do not leave ourselves at the mercy of our memories or the crisis of the moment.

The tools we use to keep track of our priorities need not be burdensome or expensive. Some people work well with daily planners; others operate best with notebooks. Inscribing priorities on scrap or loose-leaf sheets of paper is acceptable, providing we do not lose or scatter them. What is essential is that we have an organized system that works for us. Experiment with these different priority-recording systems until you find one that you feel comfortable with.

Working with the Pareto Principle

There is a rule of thumb in many activities that operates according to the ratio of 80/20. Members of many an organization have commented that 80 percent of the work is done by 20 percent of the people. Our concern is with the 80/20 rule, more commonly known as the *Pareto Principle,* as it applies to projects and activities. Vilfredo Pareto, a nineteenth-century economist, is given credit for observing that a majority of our efforts yield a minority of results, and vice versa. Whatever the actual percentages are, experience verifies that there are many situations in which actual results are substantially disproportionate to the efforts applied. Certain efforts bear little fruit, at least on the surface, while other activities reward us with generous dividends, with no measurable pattern or correlation between efforts and results.

It would be nice if we could master the Pareto Principle, and make it work to our advantage. We could channel our efforts in an efficient and effective direction, and eliminate many of our frustrations, disappointments, blind alleys, and thankless tasks. In our imperfect world, the best we can hope for is to keep this principle in mind when planning and prioritizing, and try to devote our prime energy and resources to what we perceive as the productive 20 percent of our tasks. It may be possible to eliminate some of the less productive 80 percent activities by deferring them; eventually they might prove to be unnecessary.

We would be naive to think that the majority of activities could or indeed should be eliminated or transformed into the more gratifying 20 percent of activities. Much of this 80 percent of activities is simply foundational or grunt work that must be done. The key is to distinguish the necessary grunt work from the borderline, nonessential tasks, and prioritize accordingly. By striving for excellence rather than perfection, we can frequently distinguish dispensable tasks from essential ones.

Although our judgment of the efficacy of tasks can improve with experience, there will always be a learning curve and an element of uncertainty and surprise. The objective of prioritizing is to direct our efforts in a responsible manner, and accept the results with grace, resourcefulness, and perseverance. We can apply the Pareto Principle to the prioritizing process as a tool for evaluating the potential benefit to be derived from performance of the activity. Spending a majority of our efforts on the preparatory or foundational activities is a form of education and experience, a sometimes grueling prerequisite of learning and achievement. We can try to identify and emphasize the most important and urgent tasks in both the gratifying (20 percent) and grunt work (80 percent) categories, while deferring or even eliminating activities that are less crucial to the achievement of our objectives.

Living with Unfinished Business

One of the most anxiety-producing aspects of prioritizing and modern life in general is the nagging presence of unfinished business. Put simply, our work is never done. We usually do not accomplish all of our objectives over a given period of time. Perhaps our expectations and estimations are mistaken, or events transpire that divert us from our course. The end result is the same: the comforting sense of completion that we naturally desire continues to elude us. In a sense, unfinished business is symbolic of life: When one challenge ends, another begins.

Unless we cope with unfinished business in a constructive manner, it can discourage and wear us down. Let us reflect together on how we can live with unfinished business in a healthy way.

Self-Inflicted Pressure

Much of the anxiety we experience over unfinished business stems from pressure we put on ourselves. Often our expectations are overly ambitious or unrealistic. Sometimes things beyond our control happen, and we become angry and uptight. Whatever the circumstances, there is usually an element of self-induced pressure. We can identify unnecessary anxiety by considering whether or not we are reacting out of proportion to the situation. Do the prospective consequences merit our reaction? Sometimes it helps to consider the worst consequence of the unfinished business. Is it worth getting worked up over?

We can also look at the flip side of unfinished business: prospective positive consequences. Are we distorting the picture by focusing solely on the perceived negative consequences? Would a balanced outlook yield greater objectivity and less anxiety?

Anxiety over unfinished business intensifies any tendencies toward procrastination. It arouses fear, magnifies nuances, distorts perceptions, and diffuses our energy. The key is to view the consequences of and circumstances leading up to unfinished business as they really are. We set and perform our priorities as best we can, and deal with the consequences and loose ends with poise and resourcefulness. Unfinished business does not merit an ulcer or heart attack. The work will be there tomorrow, so we must do our part to make sure we are there to tackle it. We might even be so bold as to think: "So what! Everything didn't get done. Life is imperfect. I'm frustrated and a little angry, so I'll find some constructive way of channeling these emotions. If I have to absorb negative consequences, I'll deal with them as best I can. It's not worth getting sick."

Pressure from Others

Anxiety over unfinished business is often a reaction to the pressure others put on us, whether at work or at home. While we cannot control their words and actions, we can control our own. Because such external pressure can also be harmful to the perpetrator, we do them no favor by caving in to it. With patience, poise, resolve, and thoughtful actions and communications, we may even be able to influence them to act in a less severe fashion.

Arguing or direct confrontation usually stirs controversy and intransigence. The most effective approach is to respond to another's intensity or anxiety in a calm, controlled manner. Do not let them dictate the rules and play the game on their turf; try to find a neutral ground where both parties must rely less on defensive or offensive strategy than on consensus building.

Coping with the external pressures that accompany unfinished business requires different communication approaches depending upon the person and situation. The process of developing a communication strategy usually includes private reflection and analysis, brainstorming, and consultation of a trustworthy sounding board and objective observer with experience in such matters.

The same principle discussed in reference to self-inflicted anxiety applies to pressure from others. While we respect their viewpoints, and want to accommodate others as much as possible, we cannot do more than our best. If we have made a sincere attempt to fulfill the reasonable expectations of others, there is no need for anxiety or guilt. If they overreact to something, our getting caught up in the frenzy only makes it worse for everybody. Conversely, if their frustration is justified, we should be quick to own up to our responsibility and do our best to make amends.

Anxiety over unfinished business ties in with our frustration over not being in complete control of our destiny. The work and burdens will be there tomorrow whether we like it or not. It is prudent to do the best we can, and leave the rest to providence and the events that come our way, not in our imagination or worries, but in reality.

Unfinished business may hang over our heads, but it does not have to depress or derail us. While unfinished business will sometimes bring unpleasant consequences, chronic worry and anxiety only exacerbate the situation. A sense of humor and perspective can go a long way toward preserving our health and sanity while helping us make prudent judgments in the midst of ambiguous and intense situations.

Conclusion

Prioritizing is the systematic ordering of tasks and activities. It helps us channel our energies, abilities, and resources in an appropriate direction. We can improve our prioritizing judgments and intuition by learning from our mistakes and experiences, and growing in self-knowledge. The following are guidelines and reminders from our discussion of prioritizing.

The *ABC*s of Priorities

1. Do not let unfinished business hang over you like a dark cloud; even if you mismanage tasks or activities, *there is more to life than efficiency.*

2. Utilize the *ABC* nomenclature for distinguishing levels of priorities based upon urgency and importance.
   a. Rank your priorities within each category: *A*—Must do; *B*—Preferably do; *C*—Maybe do.
   b. Write down activities associated with each priority. Schedule *A* activities first, then *B* and *C*.
   c. Keep your documentation of each category separate so as to avoid confusion.
   d. When you get discouraged with a task, do not go automatically to a *B* or *C* task. A break may be necessary, or you can go to another *A* task. An *A* task

with therapeutic or energizing effects is an ideal alternative. Sometimes *C* priorities can be therapeutic and are worthwhile. Ask the question: If I do this *C* priority, how far will it set me back from accomplishing my *A* priorities? Will its therapeutic benefits actually help me in the long run?

  e. Rank reading material by *A*, *B*, and *C* priority levels.

3. Develop daily "to do" lists the day before (or earlier), and review them in the morning and upon completion of the day.

  a. Cross items off your list as completed. Derive a sense of satisfaction from their completion. Give yourself simple rewards (and when warranted, major rewards) on a consistent basis for working through your priorities list. Reward efforts as much as results.

  b. Determine the resolution of leftover items and go calmly about your business.

4. Try not to schedule unrelated minor tasks for the same time period unless you have established (at least mentally) precise objectives and completion timetables for those tasks. Such tasks can very easily acquire a life of their own, resulting in unnecessary inefficiency.

5. Rotate tasks to break the monotony. Preferably the respective tasks will involve different skills.

6. Do your *A* priorities in the time of day when you function best.

  a. For activities involving others, either inquire about or estimate their "prime time."

7. The less time you feel you have for prioritizing, the more important it probably is. Our perception that we lack time means that we should take time to plan.

  a. By failing to plan, you will have trouble distinguishing between *A*, *B*, and *C* priorities, especially under pressure.

8. Devote time, energy, and resources in proportion to an activity's importance.
   a. Consciously exploit the 80/20 rule. Ask the question: What tasks will get 80 percent of the work done in 20 percent of the time? Schedule those first.
   b. By doing the most productive tasks first, you may be able to eliminate some of the remaining tasks.
   c. Beware of getting bogged down in grunt work. Become conscious of situations where you are devoting excess precious resources to secondary priorities. Consider how you might reduce the time necessary to accomplish these tasks.

9. Discern when perfectionism is important, and when it is counterproductive.
   a. Be conscious of the trap of overdoing tasks. For example, informal letters or memos need not be literary masterpieces.
   b. Keep in mind the principle of marginal utility (that is, the results or usefulness of incremental efforts). Recognize when the law of diminishing returns takes effect.

10. Keep long-term objectives in mind even when doing a small task. Are your daily and weekly activities bringing you closer to your desired destination? If not, are the reasons acceptable to you?

Reflection Exercises

Do you use a daily planning system that works for you? Would your effectiveness and organization benefit from a change in method or materials?

Do you distinguish between *A, B,* and *C* priorities?

Do you consciously remember the Pareto Principle (80/20 results/efforts or efforts/results rule) in planning your work and home schedule?

Sample Prioritizing Format

"To Do" Key:

Priority Code (PC)—*A, B, C*

Task Reminders

Appointments, meetings, deadlines, projects, rewards, telephone calls to make and receive, correspondence to send and receive.

Week of _____

Short-Term and Long-Term Goals

_____   _____

_____   _____

_____   _____

PC	Task	PC	Task
Monday	Date _____		
—	_____	—	_____
—	_____	—	_____
—	_____	—	_____
—	_____	—	_____
—	_____	—	_____
Tuesday	Date _____		
—	_____	—	_____
—	_____	—	_____
—	_____	—	_____
—	_____	—	_____
—	_____	—	_____

Wednesday   Date _____

___   _____   ___   _____
___   _____   ___   _____
___   _____   ___   _____
___   _____   ___   _____
___   _____   ___   _____

Thursday   Date _____

___   _____   ___   _____
___   _____   ___   _____
___   _____   ___   _____
___   _____   ___   _____
___   _____   ___   _____

Friday   Date _____

___   _____   ___   _____
___   _____   ___   _____
___   _____   ___   _____
___   _____   ___   _____
___   _____   ___   _____

Saturday   Date _____

___   _____   ___   _____
___   _____   ___   _____
___   _____   ___   _____
___   _____   ___   _____
___   _____   ___   _____

Sunday   Date _____

___   _____   ___   _____
___   _____   ___   _____
___   _____   ___   _____
___   _____   ___   _____
___   _____   ___   _____

Pending and Upcoming Tasks

— _____   — _____
— _____   — _____
— _____   — _____
— _____   — _____
— _____   — _____

Source: *Personal Energy Manager* (a time, activities, and energy planner developed by Karl Schultz and published by Genesis Personal Development Center).

Reflections, Applications, and Little Victories

2

Developing a Personal and Professional Rhythm: Pace, Patterns, and Patience

Pace

Even in the midst of the modern rat race, we can exert some control over the speed at which we work and live. Just as there are certain times in the day when we operate at peak efficiency, so there is a certain pace at which we proceed most effectively. We can discover this pace if we observe and experiment with our speed and intensity at home and at work until we find the right rhythm. In many cases, it simply involves taking our time, thinking before we act, and becoming more aware of what is going on inside and around us, including the results and consequences of our tempo and actions. We may have to alternate our speed and intensity temporarily according to the needs of others and circumstances, but over the long haul we can find a pace that is healthy and effective for us. To do this, we must observe the consequences of our actions at different paces and intensity levels, and gradually gravitate toward a daily rhythm that suits us.

Gandhi was prophetic in observing that there is more to life than increasing its speed. In many cases, steady and easy does the job just fine. When we act as if everything has to be rushed, we grind ourselves and others down. It is important to take time daily to observe the fruits of our labors, our effect on others, the rate of our breath and heartbeat, and our mental and emotional state. We can then fine-tune our efforts and intensity level to suit the task and circumstances at hand.

Personal Patterns

Because of the routine and repetitive nature of many of our daily tasks, it is beneficial for us to develop a practical rhythm in performing them. This means developing standard, but not inflexible, patterns for completing routine tasks without reinventing the wheel and wasting time and energy. Most of us already follow specific routines or patterns, either consciously or unconsciously. It is helpful to assess periodically whether or not those patterns can be improved.

Typical opportunities for developing patterns or standard routines are morning, bedtime, mealtime, and during perfunctory and repetitive tasks. Through reflection and careful planning, we can enter into an efficient rhythm in performing these tasks that will help us complete them in a timely manner.

Performing personal and professional mundane tasks in an effective manner is an ongoing process of observation, assessment, and adjustment. Monitoring of personal and professional patterns requires patience, reflection, and analysis. This process need not be complex or overly rigorous. It can be as simple as writing the various steps we take in completing a specific routine, and considering some modification to our procedure that would save time or energy, and perhaps yield improved results. As situations, resources, and aptitudes change, so can the best way to perform our routine tasks.

Patience

One of the by-products of our high-tech world of instant results and growing convenience has been a gradual disappearance of the virtue of patience. You do not often find popular self-help books by either Christian or secular authors on the topic of patience. One exception is the inspiring and practical book by Reverend Valentino del Mazza, *The Patience of God*. Patience is important because it contributes to our health and effectiveness. It is developed through desire, maturation, and faith; we must believe that good things are worth waiting for, and that the process of learning patience has intrinsic value. Patience is learned more through experience than through words; it does not require explanation as much as application.

As a practical exercise, take time to gauge your patience in various situations. How often do you try to make decisions or resolve dilemmas prematurely, based on insufficient resources or information? Do you utilize your intuition and sense of timing? How often do you get upset about situations beyond your control instead of responding to them in a reasonable and constructive manner? Are there times when you would be better off accepting, coping, adjusting, and moving on, instead of resisting? We can observe our reactions to events and people on a periodic basis to gauge our degree of patience.

Conclusion

Patience, personal patterns, and pace work together to create a healthy and effective rhythm at home and at work. We can develop these through desire, attention, hard work, and persistence. Perhaps we know someone who embraces life and work with a healthy, relaxed attitude, relating to people and events in a rational and mature manner. We might ask them how they were able to develop a healthy rhythm. While each person's circumstances are unique, there is a common wisdom about life that we can share with each other. Let us continue our quest to maintain a healthy pace and intensity level at work and at home. In some small way, we can make progress (that is, attain little victories) every day. In the next chapter, we explore a complementary but often ignored virtue: presence.

Reflection Exercises

Are there any areas at work or home where I need to pace myself better, perhaps altering the speed and intensity at which I operate?

Do I perform routine activities in an efficient manner? Can I make any improvements to the patterns I follow in specific situations and time periods?

In which areas or circumstances am I typically impatient? Is there a cost to my impatience? How might I become more patient and pliable?

What aspects or activities of my lifestyle and workstyle contribute to a rhythm of wellness and effectiveness? Which seem to have a detrimental effect? Discuss.

Reflections, Applications, and Little Victories

3

Presence to the Present

L et us begin by defining what we mean by the phrase "presence to the present." *Presence* is a personal stance of receptivity, vitality, and awareness in mind, body, and spirit, to the world around you. It is a fundamental communication posture, both in personal and professional relationships. Presence is essential to marital and other family relationships, as well as to peer and hierarchical relationships at work. How many times have we been in conversation with someone whose mind and heart seemed to be elsewhere? How often have we been guilty of the same? Presence to the present is the lived art of giving other people or tasks the attention and effort they deserve. This is captured in the ancient Latin saying *age quod agis,* translated as "do what you are doing." Pay attention to the here and now; concentrate on those variables and factors most directly in your control at the present moment. There is a time and place best suited for dealing with the past, the future, and other factors out of our control.

Presence is being available in body, mind, and spirit to whatever life brings before us in the present moment. We are not living in the past or dwelling on the future. Chronic guilt and anxiety drain us of energy we could use in the present moment.

There is very little literature in the training and development field on the importance of presence. There are many excellent workshops, programs, and books about listening and communication skills, yet few of them deal substantively with the issue of presence. This void is attributable to its whole-person, existential, and nonempirical quality, and the emphasis business professionals place on analytical issues and ideas, immediate and tangible concerns, and material realities. Presence is a product of the heart as much as of the body and mind, and its influence is felt in subtle but significant ways. The economic imbalances and social injustices that permeate western culture's materialistic approach to business testify to the need for an infusion of compassion, sensitivity, and integrity, and a renewed commitment to the common good through attention to environmental, social, and family issues. So many complicated listening and communication skills programs would be superfluous if we focused instead on such fundamentals as presence, precision, sincerity, patience, understanding, and respect.

Biblical Counsels

Presence in body, mind, and spirit to the present moment is a continuous process of sincere receptivity to life and God's will. In fact, it is the opposite of what most best-selling time management and human potential gurus tell us. Secular proponents speak of taking control of our lives, while God asks us to integrate integrity of effort with trust in providence. Worthy of meditation is Christ's discussion of worry, human limitations, and providence in the Gospels of Matthew and Luke (cf. Mt 6:25–34; Lk 12:22–31). The Lord himself, no stranger to the potential of nature and grace, tells us that each day has trouble enough of its own. So why are we going beyond the present moment when it holds enough challenges to occupy all of our energy?

If we are looking beyond the present moment, our energy becomes diffuse and our attentions distracted, and we can create even more problems. We cannot be sure that tomorrow will come for ourselves, our loved ones, or those we encounter, so in a natural, humble way, why not live each day like it is our last? This is the opposite of the "do it all with gusto, eat, drink, and be merry" manipulative advertising slogans of Madison Avenue. Qoheleth, the author of Ecclesiastes, counsels us to enjoy life just the same, but within the context of a healthy respect for God and his will. We might even call

Qoheleth the Bible's wise guy: He is in touch with, and at times discouraged by, the difficulties of life. However, this does not stop him from living and enjoying life to the fullest, while continuing to ask questions about God, himself, and life. He is the spiritual source of the following maxims: there's a time and place (season) for everything (cf. Eccl 3:1–9), and there's nothing new under the sun (cf. Eccl 1:9). If Qoheleth were with us today, I believe he would be both amused and saddened by our frantic pace, grasping ambition, and idolization of vanities. Slow down, he might say, and be where you are, do what you are doing, and do not let the endless array of personal growth books, counsels, and platitudes overwhelm you (cf. Eccl 12:11–12).

Ways of Developing Presence

How do we develop presence? No surprises here: exercise, spiritual reading (or *lectio divina*), quality time with nature, breathing or awareness exercises (especially those by Anthony de Mello), writing in a personal journal, and daily quiet time. For people with hectic schedules, try making a commitment to three minutes of quiet time, twice a day; you can always increase the time, but you cannot excuse yourself from the practice because of time pressures. If we cannot fit in six minutes on most days (everybody has out-of-control days occasionally), then our schedule needs a massage before it rubs us the wrong way for good.

Within the Catholic tradition, the spiritual path of Saint Thérèse of Lisieux, described as the "Little Way," offers testimony to the power of living one day, activity, encounter, trial at a time. Her autobiographical journal, *Autobiography of a Saint: The Story of a Soul,* is an inspirational testimony to the spiritual efficacy of attention to little victories and the mundane tasks of daily life.

Presence to the present is also a natural by-product of healthy attitudes and behavior in our relationships. A frequent comment made about Popes John Paul II and Paul VI was that when they shook your hand and looked you in the eyes they gave you the sense that you were the only person who existed for them at that moment. Their internalized value of respect for people naturally manifested itself in their interpersonal interactions.

A Voice Worth Hearing

I recommend that individuals interested in developing a greater sense of presence in their life review the books, videotapes, and audiotapes of Father Anthony de Mello, a Jesuit psychotherapist and spiritual director from India who died in 1987.

I have not found a comparable resource for practical, down-to-earth, nonmaterialistic wisdom about human development. In addition to being substantive and inspirational, Father de Mello is highly entertaining and dynamic, both as a speaker and writer, with a special aptitude for storytelling. He weaves insights into human nature from many of the world's major religions and cultures with observations gleaned from psychology and the human potential movement, as well as from his experiences in counseling, spiritual direction, and teaching. Especially helpful are the imaginative, yet highly practical, exercises he proposes in his earliest works, *Sadhana* and *Wellsprings,* and in his videotape program, *A Way to God for Today,* produced by Tabor.

Father de Mello is a master at helping individuals enjoy and utilize their five senses in a healthy and developmental manner. Those who knew, studied under, and worked with Father de Mello speak respectfully and fondly about him, and lament the void his death has left both personally and in the personal growth and spirituality fields. For people interested in wellness, self-knowledge, stress management, and human relationship dynamics, Father de Mello can serve as a competent and enjoyable guide.

In our next chapter, we continue the theme of communication skills by focusing on the role persuasion can play in our effort to be effective managers of our gifts, resources, and opportunities.

Sources for Inspiration from Anthony de Mello, S.J.

Books

Awareness: The Perils and Opportunities of Reality. New York: Image Books, 1990.

Contact with God. Chicago: Loyola University Press, 1991.

More One Minute Nonsense. Chicago: Loyola University Press, 1993.

One Minute Nonsense. Chicago: Loyola University Press, 1992.

One Minute Wisdom. New York: Image Books, 1988.

Sadhana: A Way to God. New York: Image Books, 1984.

The Song of the Bird. New York: Image Books, 1984.

Taking Flight: A Book of Story-Meditations. New York: Doubleday, 1988.

Wellsprings. New York: Image Books, 1986.

Also of interest: Valles, Carlos G., S.J. *Mastering Sadhana: On Retreat with Anthony de Mello*. New York: Image Books, 1987.

Audiocassette Programs

De Mello Satellite Retreat. St. Louis, Mo.: We and God Spirituality Center, 1989.

Sadhana: A Way to God. St. Louis, Mo.: We and God Spirituality Center, 1984.

Wake Up to Life. St. Louis, Mo.: We and God Spirituality Center, 1989.

Wellsprings. St. Louis, Mo.: We and God Spirituality Center, 1986.

Reflection Exercises

In what circumstances do I typically lack presence? During which activities do I seem to be someplace else? Why?

What small steps can I take to be more present to people, tasks, and events?

In what areas of my life am I not living in the present? What are my real reasons for escaping from reality?

What small steps can I take to re-enter the present despite my pain?

Presence to the Present Journal

Area (where I lack sufficient presence to the present):

Desired Growth:

Strategy (for example, modification of attitude or behavior, or redirection of energy):

Area:

Desired Growth:

Strategy:

Area:

Desired Growth:

Strategy:

Reflections, Applications, and Little Victories

4

Persuasion: The Art of Engaging the Support and Cooperation of Others

B ookstores are filled with books offering practical advice on how to win friends, influence people, and manage situations. Much research and publishing has been done on the art and science of persuasion from an academic, business, and self-help perspective. Rather than duplicate these efforts, I will concentrate on a small but significant component of Personal Energy Management that I have experienced to be pivotal. It is articulated in the biblical expression, "Ask and it will be given to you; seek and you will find; knock and the door will be opened to you" (Mt 7:7). I would like to add a corollary and modify that adage based on my experience: "You will not always receive what you ask (but sometimes you will, and often when you least expect it), you will enter plenty of blind alleys while you are seeking, and the door will slam in your face as well as open up to you." Persistence and persuasion can be double-edged swords; they yield admirers and rewards, but can also lead into dead ends, wayward paths, and hard lessons.

Persistence in Persuasion

No one achieves a worthwhile goal alone. We need plenty of help along the way, not only from our loved ones, friends, and peers, but from acquaintances as well. Thankfully, most people want to help others, and when given the opportunity, will extend themselves to various degrees. Recognizing that people differ in both their capacity and willingness to help, we can frame our request in such a way that we impose on others as little as necessary, and invite them to cooperate within their boundaries and preferences.

The more sincere and reasonable our request, the greater the likelihood of our receiving a positive response. The simpler we keep our proposals, the easier other people find it to comply. We cannot expect others to read our minds or between the lines.

The Purpose of Persuasion

Persuasion is not simply a means of getting our own way, but of working together with others toward the common good. There is an old French expression, *Des convaincus, pas de vaincus,* that translates as follows: "No one should feel defeated, but everyone should be persuaded."

There are many resources available for guiding and advising us on proper and effective ways of communicating with and persuading others. We can consult these according to our needs and the situation. The best resources essentially elaborate on the following principle: Listen and speak to the whole person, paying attention to the person's actions and manner as well as his words. The objective of persuasion is to communicate and cooperate freely with others in pursuit of a defined objective, and to persist in our worthwhile efforts in the face of obstacles and disappointments. The process of personal growth and effectiveness is a long and arduous one. May we find trustworthy companions and guides for our journey.

In the next chapter, we provide a practical context for the communication principles we have been discussing by considering the role of administrative skills in channeling our energy and potential.

Reflection Exercises

Which current or prospective projects or situations might benefit from my asking for assistance and cooperation? How might I go about enlisting support?

When enlisting the support of others, do I generally use the soft or hard sell? Which seems to work better?

Cite past or present experiences that influenced your response to the preceding question.

Is there any aspect of my communication and persuasion style (for example: tone, timing, approach, or language) that I would like to modify and improve?

Are there individuals with whom I can network and build mutually beneficial relationships? What steps can I take to go about this?

Reflections, Applications, and Little Victories

5

Working Smart: Organizational Skills— Desk, File, and Phone Management

Desk and File Management

Whether at work or at home, management of one's incoming and outgoing mail and administrative responsibilities can be time and energy consuming. As with most aspects of Personal Energy Management, the simpler we make our task, the fewer complications we invite—there will be enough complications without our assistance.

Simplicity must be applied to all aspects of desk management: bill paying, reminder notes, incoming and outgoing mail, and daily task items. The central concepts are effectiveness and efficiency: Do everything in its proper order and with minimal paper shuffling. Each individual must arrive at a neatness comfort level where they can operate most effectively. It is important for us to avoid clutter, to know where we put things so that we have easy access to them when necessary, and to have some system for sorting and filing papers.

The popular maxim is to handle each piece of paper just once, but this can be modified according to circumstances. In cases of incomplete information or pending events, some items may require several reviews prior to disposition. The key is to act immediately on documents of trivial or minor importance when we are 95 percent certain as to their proper disposition. The more important the document, the more scrutiny and certainty it merits. The criteria used in prioritizing, such as urgency, importance, and materiality, can help us determine the degree of care with which each item should be handled.

Sometimes it helps to make a rough sketch of our desk and file space, and then write in where we think items should be placed. We want to be sure there is sufficient uncluttered space on our desk, with clearly distinguished piles containing incoming and outgoing mail, bills, daily task items, and reminder notes. Stacking trays can be helpful for maintaining different groupings of documentation. Once we experiment with various layouts and arrive at an effective scheme, we must stick with it until the need or opportunity for modification or improvement arises. The more disciplined we are in adhering to our desk management, the less likely it is that we will lose or forget items, and the more fluidly we will complete our tasks.

There is no one filing system that is right for everyone. Experiment and refine until you come up with a workable system. The following are sample categories for a filing system:

Bank statements, retirement accounts, purchase receipts, warranty papers, medical papers, identification papers (for example: birth certificate, passport), utility bills, credit card bills and documentation, directions and travel information, important miscellaneous documentation, tax receipts and filing information, personal enjoyment, remembrances, hobby information or receipts, work-related papers (this can consist of many subdivisions), incoming mail on which you are undecided and is not urgent, automobile documentation, insurance papers, newspaper or magazine articles, keepsake correspondence, humorous articles or items, brochures, government papers, social or community life items, and deadline offers.

It may be worthwhile to invest in a sturdy and sufficiently large filing space complete with hanging folders and file name tags. There can be overlap between desk and file management for certain borderline items. Some papers we may wish to keep on our desk and in view temporarily, and at a certain time relegate them to the files. Periodically, both our files and desks merit a good cleaning, with outdated or superfluous papers being thrown away. Occasionally we will throw away an item that we will need later. Because our judgments on disposition and retention are based on imperfect information, this is inevitable. Our objective is to strike a balance between being a pack rat and prematurely dispensing of work or personal items.

Phone Management

The telephone is one of the crucial elements of modern society. Unfortunately, effective and courteous telephone practices are in the minority in both personal and professional environments. While much of what we talk about in this section may seem basic, it is amazing how many people fail to abide by these principles.

One of the cardinal violations of phone ethics in today's society is the conscious failure of individuals to return telephone calls. Businesspeople will choose not to return calls because they do not want to bother with people who they doubt can help them at the present time. This is both rude and strategically questionable. The return call can be kept brief, or it can be handled by a secretary or assistant, but at least it is an acknowledgment. We never know what will come of our returning a telephone call. It may not reap immediate benefits, but it is a sign of respect for the individual and an affirmation of our integrity as businesspeople. Are we in business solely for what we can get out of it, or are we in it to build up the community, as well as to make a living? Returning phone calls is a courteous and effective business and personal practice.

Phone Image

We project an image of ourselves both personally and professionally through our use of the telephone. In order to assess how you might appear to others, you can ask yourself the following questions: Do I speak in a clear and pleasant tone of voice? Do I conduct my conversations in a relaxed manner? Do I interrupt verbally or mentally as a matter of course, or do I let others finish their thoughts? Am I willing to share a laugh or friendly remark when the situation calls for it? Do I offer the individual the help or information they need without them having to drag it from me? Do I communicate clearly the purpose of the call, and am I sensitive to the time pressures that may be on the other individual?

Phone Preparation

Do you prepare for a telephone conversation by anticipating scenarios or reactions that might arise? Do you prepare calm, reasoned responses as an alternative to being caught off guard? It often pays to take a minute or two to write down your objectives for the call, and any strategies or positions to take in response to negotiating ploys or emotional outbursts. I also like to visualize myself having a positive conversation, and keep in mind a positive image of the conversation. I do not do this to manipulate the conversation or my counterpart, but to begin the dialogue with a positive attitude. The amount of energy it takes to prepare either logically or through visualization pales in comparison to the consequences of losing my cool or misspeaking. Such preparation avoids the extremes of off-the-cuff spontaneity and rigid and rote scripted responses. Preparation and poise enable us to communicate from a position of strength even when our counterpart reacts with unbridled emotion.

Phone Mechanics

It is amazing how often telephone messages are transcribed incorrectly, misinterpreted, or misplaced. A bad day can cause us to appear reluctant and inconvenienced when asked to take a message: the audacity of the caller for imposing on us to record a detailed message. Sometimes the environment around the telephone seems like a battle zone, with background noise so obtrusive that we cannot hear the other party clearly. Or there is the case of "Fumble Fingers," the individual who seems to have a difficult time holding on to the phone, subjecting us to occasional clanks and clunks while he carries on with other activities (for example: eating, toying with papers, rearranging his desk, and so on) during our conversation.

Phone efficiency consists primarily of preparation, straightforwardness, using downtime effectively, and combining callbacks. For example, when we anticipate waiting on hold for long periods of time, it may be efficient to do administrative tasks that do not divert us from the conversation.

From an efficiency standpoint, callbacks require three considerations: the urgency of the call, the best time to reach the caller, and which calls can be returned during a designated callback period. Usually it is best to handle callbacks in a consolidated, rather than a piecemeal fashion, especially when the interruptions are quite frequent. There are times when it is both convenient and prudent to have calls held and messages taken: If we are in the middle of an important task or meeting, it may be difficult to give the conversation the attention it deserves.

Phone Checklist

The following can serve as guidelines and reminders for using the telephone in a courteous and effective manner:

☎ Never assume—write it down.

☎ Employ common sense, courtesy, etiquette, and the Golden Rule.

☎ Balance candor and straightforwardness with tact, timing, and sensitivity.

☎ Pay attention to tone, grammar, and language.

☎ Be prompt.

☎ Ensure mutual understanding of canned (or generic) responses.

☎ Conduct yourself with appropriate humor, cheerfulness, and professionalism.

☎ Cope firmly and rationally with rudeness and excessive persistence.

☎ Handle callbacks efficiently.

☎ Practice preparation, naturalness, and succinctness.

☎ Restate and confirm the mutual understanding or resolution.

☎ Listen intently; Pay attention and keep your mind on the conversation.

☎ Avoid rigid responses and scripts: Nobody likes a manipulative sales pitch or a parroting of the company line.

☎ Avoid phone phoniness: Say what you mean, and mean what you say. Insincere game playing eventually backfires. No one can legitimately fault you for being yourself if you use appropriate discretion and prudence.

☎ Be wary of saying intense things that are more appropriate for in-person conversation; err on the side of discretion.

☎ Leave a positive impression and feeling when possible.

Reflections, Applications, and Little Victories

Personal Energy Management *P* Parameters
Review and Preview

Part two of this book highlights various topics that can help us fine-tune our effectiveness on a daily basis. These practical considerations build on the principles articulated in part one, and inevitably lead us to various obstacles to effective Personal Energy Management. In part three, we examine some of the common patterns of Personal Energy Mismanagement and suggest how we might overcome or neutralize them.

Review

Principles
Philosophy
Prayer and Providence
Perspective and Poise
Purpose
Self-Knowledge and Discernment
Perseverance and Prudence

Practices
Priorities
Personal Rhythm: Pace, Patience, and Patterns
Presence to the Present
Persuasion
Desk, File, and Phone Management

Preview

Possibilities and Pitfalls
Procrastination
Perfectionism
Punctuality
Rediscovering Leisure

Part Three

Personal Energy Mismanagement Patterns

1

Procrastination

P rocrastination is a topic that is easy to put off. It is an issue for anyone who is confronted with what they perceive to be unpleasant, intimidating, or boring tasks. Who would be anxious to experience perceived negative consequences from engaging in certain activities? In this chapter, we deal with procrastination solely from a pragmatic standpoint; that is, how to get started on unpleasant tasks and eventually bring them to completion. We will defer the complex psychological issues that may underlie chronic procrastination to the appropriate authorities and resources. Our objective is to deal with procrastination from a practical perspective, and explore helpful hints for making our tasks seem less daunting.

Getting Started

The best place to start is at the beginning; with procrastination, this entails viewing the situation from an objective standpoint. Our first step is to take stock of ourselves and our situation. We try to understand our fears, worries, and hesitations over beginning the project or task. How do our personal tendencies, temperament, past experiences, and the dynamics of the situation influence our behavior? Are our concerns well founded, or have we blown them out of proportion? Are our expectations and perceptions significantly overstated or understated?

Such discernment is usually enhanced by analyzing the situation in writing. For example, we can list pros and cons or best- and worst-case scenarios, and perhaps enlist the aid of a confidant, coach, or counselor. Getting things out into the open and onto paper aids our objectivity, and takes us away from the mental and emotional merry-go-round that often accompanies procrastination.

Framing the Issues and the Activity

Perhaps there is a way of viewing the activity before us in a less intimidating way that yields itself to gradual, constructive action. Sometimes it helps to consider the worst possible consequences of our performance of the task along with the rewards that could ensue. Frequently, the feared consequences that impede us from starting on the activity turn out to be empty threats or exaggerations born of imagination or negative experiences. A balanced outlook keeps the activity in the proper perspective.

The challenge is to conceive of and frame the activity and possible consequences in such a way that we are drawn to a desired response. Such positive and motivational associations are available through proactive visualization and mental imaging. We ascribe a negative feeling, image, or sensory reaction to procrastination, and a positive feeling, image, or sensory reaction to actual performance of the instant tasks. The association can be rooted in reality or in imagination. This creative channeling of the will is not done subliminally or manipulatively. It helps us deal more responsibly with reality by recognizing the likely consequences of our actions in advance, and summoning the resources of the whole person to help us thwart bad habits.

Visualizing these consequences in vivid terms, in conjunction with our mind, body, and sensate capacities, can provide us with motivation to act, rather than procrastinate. Imagining both the rewards and negative consequences gives us a preview of the anticipated results of whichever course we take, thereby providing us with additional information and motivation for our decision. Thus, we enlist the aid of our subconscious mind in a conscious, self-directed way.

Like everything else in Personal Energy Management, our efforts and methods are judged by the criteria of Christian morality and spirituality. For example, we could creatively and legitimately associate a foul odor with a particular temptation to procrastinate, but associating performance of the act with an immoral activity would be replacing one inappropriate behavior with another.

Instant Tasks

The best way to begin a daunting endeavor is by wading in. What are some simple, instant tasks that can get us started? We can brainstorm manageable, incremental tasks that will get us moving toward our goal and provide some momentum and confidence. We can then build on our progress by brainstorming additional instant tasks. Breaking a project down into manageable parts usually helps to take away the aura of impossibility.

Patience and Charity Begin with Ourselves

"For the just man falls seven times and rises again. . . ." (Prv 24:16). One of the worst things we can do when we procrastinate is chastise ourselves harshly. When we waste time or perform below expectations, it is important to be gentle with ourselves in acknowledging our error and resolving to improve in the future.

Preserving Your Options

Some personal growth authors advocate cutting off all escape routes as a deterrent to procrastination. Artificially reducing the temptation only suppresses and defers the underlying issues. This engages the negative tendency of human nature to eradicate or eliminate problems rather than understand, reframe, or resolve them! Such bridge burning backfires when circumstances evolve to where the escape route becomes necessary.

Individuals who work poorly under pressure may need the security of an escape route. They may need to wean themselves from procrastinating tendencies in a gentle, nonthreatening manner.

There will be times when our escape routes will be cut off or diminished naturally, and we have to begin the task out of sheer necessity or urgency. Rather than artificially induce such pressure, it is more prudent to work with the circumstances as they are, preserving all options and utilizing all resources, thereby avoiding both extremes of looking for an easy way out or of unnecessarily forcing the issue.

A final technique for empowering ourselves in the battle against procrastination is that of creating a positive environment in which to perform the task. Brainstorm ways of modifying and orchestrating controllable external factors to make the activity less intimidating. Procrastination is a formidable foe against which we should summon all of our resources; optimizing the external environment and variable factors can encourage us to begin on the task. For example, we must get rid of unnecessary distractions and outlets until we have the self-discipline to resist them. Make your physical surroundings conducive to performance by making them reasonably, but not excessively, comfortable.

Just Say No

An internal compulsion to please others or to avoid confrontation can increase our vulnerability to procrastination. It is best to avoid the extremes of either automatically saying no or of saying yes for fear of disappointing the requester. If you are going to say no to someone, tell them immediately. This courtesy helps them look for alternative sources of assistance. If you are not sure, you can always give a conditional response as long as you are clear in expressing the uncertain nature of your ability to help. Be as precise as possible, and do not unduly assume. The human ability to read minds and interpret nuances declines significantly when we are under duress. Tension and confusion cloud and impede our faculties.

An important aspect of discerning the appropriate response to a request is knowing our decision-making criteria, as well as our capabilities and limitations. Many well-meaning people mislead others with a "yes" because they do not know themselves or their discernment criteria well enough to make a mature decision. By *discernment criteria* we mean the values, beliefs, and principles that guide us in making what we feel is the right choice.

When yes and no become crossed, we make procrastination a more complicated issue for ourselves and others. The ultimate objective is to say yes when you mean yes, and no when you mean no. It is better to be conservative and pleasantly surprise someone than to be careless with our "yes" and cause unnecessary disappointment and even resentment. In the next chapter, we spend time on perhaps the most pivotal of the Personal Energy Management parameters, perfectionism, which contains seeds of growth as well as stagnation and frustration.

Reflection Exercises

Which routine tasks involve a distaste or fear that compels you to procrastinate? What underlies your reticence to complete the task(s), and how might you remedy this? (See the procrastination prevention suggestions discussed in this chapter: For example, envision positive results from performance, and negative results from procrastination.)

How do you reward yourself when you overcome procrastination tendencies? Is this sufficient to encourage similar future behavior?

Does your environment stimulate procrastination tendencies? (For example, an overly critical boss or family member, or harsh penalties for failed expectations.) Within your work or life situation, how can you prudently and gently modify either your environment, attitude, or behavior?

Do you have difficulty either saying no (pleasing) or yes (overly cautious or self-absorbed)? Are there particular situations, requests, and personalities that trigger this compulsive response, or is it an overall pattern relatively independent of circumstances? Do you sense a need to improve in this area, and if so, how?

Once we isolate and identify procrastination tendencies, we can take steps to disarm them. Are there any such tendencies you wish to confront? What practical actions, attitudes, or perspective adjustments would help you cope with, diminish, or perhaps overcome these tendencies?

Reflections, Applications, and Little Victories

2

Perfectionism: Blessing or Curse?

There may be no more difficult aspect of Personal Energy Management than the challenge of maintaining a healthy tension between the desire for excellence and a humble recognition of human imperfection and limitations. Because the word *perfectionism* generally carries negative connotations, it is important that we define it. *Perfectionism* is an obsessive desire for excellence, completion, or resolution that violates recognition and observance of behavioral norms and situational limitations. It is a virtue transformed by human weakness into a potentially destructive fault. It is the antithesis of apathy; generally, the perfectionist cares too much, and ends up overstepping boundaries.

Health and human potential authorities distinguish the desire for excellence from the compulsion to perfection. Perfectionists have difficulty making that distinction, often because of environmental conditioning or for deep-seated emotional and psychological reasons. Their dilemma is ambiguous and confusing because there are times when persistence beyond ordinary efforts and boundaries seems to pay off. People without perfectionist tendencies rarely enter into this dilemma because they are generally satisfied with average or acceptable results. Ultimately, the problem consists of unrealistic and unhealthy expectations and attitudes. The perfectionist's inner drive to achieve and perform causes him to lose perspective and self-control on issues that typically strike an emotional or experiential nerve.

When you are in relationship with another individual, how do you know when to persist in trying to work something out or when to take a break? When working on a project for a demanding customer, boss, or market, how do you know when you have reached the point of diminishing returns? Sometimes perfection seems to be demanded of us by circumstances or other people, and this feeds our compulsive tendencies. Other times we misinterpret the expectations of others or fail to communicate in a precise manner, and thereby operate under mistaken impressions. Whatever the case, the expectations of others or ourselves cannot empower us to do the impossible; the harder we try, the more anxious and frustrated we feel. Because distinguishing between excellence and perfection requires both reflection and self-control, engaging in the discernment process helps us mature and develop our self-understanding.

Perfectionism can have deep emotional roots in family systems, peer expectations, and social environments. These go far beyond the scope of our exploration. Instead, let us look at some simple, practical ways we can combat perfectionism in a healthy and even humorous manner. Humor is one of the best antidotes for perfectionism.

Perfectionism can be stimulated or exacerbated by the excessive expectations of others, particularly those in positions of authority. Whether their intentions are self-serving or well meaning, they stir up our vulnerabilities. Rather than try to change excessively demanding individuals by a frontal assault, we can gradually reform our response to their prodding. We do not have to take their expectations too seriously. We can inject reasonableness into the equation. We should seek a level of excellence that does not do violence to others or ourselves. Hopefully, they will eventually accept our refusal to participate in their circular quest for perfection, and gradually modify their expectations. This battle of wills can manifest itself in a variety of ways and levels, and may be mutually uncomfortable initially. While such forthright communications and subtle positioning requires reflection, sensitivity, courage, and timing, the resulting peace of mind is better than letting others lead you into physical and emotional ailments.

Reflection on the human condition reveals that perfection is beyond our capability. Imperfection marks everything that we do. Nothing in creation is perfect or lasts forever. Human beings are the only creatures who must deal with this on an emotional, mental, moral, and spiritual level.

It remains possible to live peacefully and effectively with the sober reality of imperfection. Letting go of our innate desire for perfection and completeness is a difficult and painful process. It requires energy and maturity on the physical, emotional, mental, spiritual, and moral levels. It begins with our decision and efforts to love and accept ourselves, people, and the world as they are, rather than as we would like them to be. Bearing in mind the little victories concept of gentle and gradual growth, we can work toward tolerance and flexibility in the dimensions mentioned above. We must channel our physical energies, feelings, attitudes, prayers, and decisions toward the ideal that we can approach, but not achieve completely: loving acceptance and submission to God's will and providence as manifested and discerned in our lives. This includes fighting injustice and correcting weaknesses and wrongs in a spirit of love, patience, respectful sensitivity, and humility.

The Spirit Is Willing, but the Flesh Is Weak

In conjunction with our best efforts and the support of others, including the church and our family, we can pray for God's help in avoiding perfectionism. The desire to transcend limits is inherited from our primordial parents, Adam and Eve, and affirmed by us. It cannot be overcome by nature alone. This is not an excuse, but a reality for which we are responsible within the capacities God has given us. We continue to be enticed by excessive behaviors and trespasses, even though Scripture and our experience tell us that the pleasures of sin and excess are temporary, and the consequences inevitable.

To use the analogy of Eden, the permissible fruit was as delightful to the eyes and senses as the forbidden fruit, with the difference being the perceived capacity of the forbidden fruit to make us wise, that is, successful and autonomous. Scripture portrays the tragic truth of human existence: Human beings created in the image of God and gifted with privileged accountability to God's beneficent Word choose to contemplate and follow the prideful provocations and deceptions of the anti-Word. It did not just happen in Eden; it relates directly to our inner compulsion to succeed on our terms, that is, radical self-will.

Rather than pursue a Promethean existence that exceeds our capacities, and, like Eve, overstate God's prohibition (cf. Gn 3:3), we can work toward being satisfied with who we are and enjoying the blessings that God wishes us to experience. Jesus ate and drank with sinners because he knew that it is not what goes into the body, but what comes out of the heart—usually exiting through our mouth, angry countenance (cf. Gn 4:5–6), and clenched fists—that destroys.

The more we progress in placing ourselves in God's hands, the more we discover not only how imperfect we are, but the beauty in ourselves and others. Eventually we can learn to quit judging others and ourselves based on our private agenda. Coping with imperfection is one of life's great challenges and struggles. It is the summit of personal and professional integration and development.

Practical Pointers for Puncturing Perfectionism

1. Try to enjoy and appreciate life as it is, rather than as your desires and agenda would have it.

2. Do not be surprised at criticism and even reprisals from those who demand the impossible. Remember that they cannot take away your will to be reasonable and poised.

3. Practice doing things 99 percent right when 100 percent correct is overkill.

4. Repeat affirmations to yourself, such as "I accept and respect the sincere efforts of myself and others."

5. Try to interact with others who expect excellence rather than perfection.

6. Keep in mind that in most cases it is more effective to do five important things 95 percent correct than one thing 100 percent. There are times when 100 percent is important, but generally these are obvious: for example, defusing or handling a bomb, or performing a delicate surgical procedure.

7. Enjoy the little things in life that are imperfect but pleasant and satisfying.

8. Read practical books on cognitive therapy, such as *A New Guide to Rational Living,* by Albert Ellis; *Feeling Good: The New Mood Therapy,* by David D. Burns; and *Love Is Never Enough,* by Aaron T. Beck.

9. Target little victories, rather than overnight changes. This is especially crucial with regards to deep-seated habits and weaknesses. Gradually develop and modify habits, behaviors, patterns, and attitudes while you understand

yourself and the roots of your problems more fully. An inordinate and hasty desire to uproot weeds can damage the soil and stifle seeds of growth.

10. Observe all the flawed people in the Bible whom God works through and accepts as they are, and who do good despite themselves.

11. Spend time with parts of nature that appeal to you, and observe with your mind, heart, and senses that the natural world is perfectly happy being imperfect. Paradise is the experience of being naked (that is, exposed, vulnerable, and real) and unashamed (that is, with no inclination or compulsion to wear masks or defenses, to demean ourselves or others, or to feebly justify ourselves or compensate for our perceived inadequacy through makeshift fig leaves).

12. Be conscious of projecting and transferring onto yourself or others your own or others' unresolved issues, insecurities, conditioned expectations, and open wounds. Never condemn or judge self-righteously. View all persons and situations, especially yourself and those closest (and therefore more vulnerable) to you, with mercy and compassion, based on an authentic and sufficient understanding of the person and situation.

In the next chapter, we discuss punctuality, a traditional virtue that sometimes accompanies perfectionism, and is an important practical manifestation of personal integrity and respect for others.

Reflection Exercises

Are there particular activities, relationships, or situations that evoke perfectionistic responses? What combination of factors influenced the development of these tendencies?

Perfectionism arises when the boundaries of excellence and healthy persistence are exceeded. We often miss the gray area between tenacity and obstinacy because some inner value compels us to ignore internal and external caution signals. Sometimes trespassing this area yields good as well as bad fruit, and our desire to succeed is abetted. Discuss your experience of this fine line, including how you would like to modify your behavior, attitude, and mental patterns in the future.

Perfectionism usually has its roots in early childhood or ado-
lescent experiences. Can you recall or identify any family,
peer, or institutional influences that may have planted the
seeds of compulsion, intolerance, obsessiveness, or anxiety?

How might you modify the excessive behaviors and unrealistic expectations that compel you to demand more of yourself
and others than is prudent and healthy? What little victories
can you claim and achieve in this area?

The causes, symptoms, effects, and remedies of perfectionism
involve the mind, body, and spirit in varying degrees. Considering these dimensions, develop a game plan for counter-
ing perfectionist tendencies. This could include modifying
mental attitudes or physical practices, reexamining anxiety-
producing values and beliefs, and monitoring our automatic
responses to stimuli that trigger perfectionistic responses.

Reflections, Applications, and Little Victories

3

Punctuality:
The Politeness of Royalty

There are times when we can do little to prevent tardiness to certain events, meetings, or gatherings. We can nonetheless practice the virtue of punctuality. *Punctuality* is a commitment to be on time in accordance with one's responsibility and word. It is a manifestation of self-discipline and of respect for the time and energy of others.

Punctuality need not be a compulsive tendency, though it can be. It is a decision and discipline that helps us interact effectively and respectfully with other people. Punctuality is particularly important today because it has become somewhat the exception rather than the rule. It is quite tempting to use the busy schedules and hectic pace of modern life as a rationalization for our tardiness. If we are not careful, excuses for tardiness can evolve into a pattern where we make increasingly less effort to be punctual.

Time Cushions

Perhaps the most common excuse for tardiness is that something important or unexpected came up. While the relative legitimacy of an excuse depends on the facts of the situation, an important consideration is whether or not the individual factored a time cushion into his schedule to allow for unforeseen circumstances.

A side benefit of such allowances is that we can use the leftover cushion time to relax, prepare ourselves for the event, meditate, pray, or simply observe or enjoy our surroundings. Because we have given ourselves a few extra minutes to allow for the unexpected, we can take our time en route and smell the roses. Conversely, if we are hassled and hurried, our attention will be focused on the traffic, queues, bureaucracy, or other obstacles to our destination.

A good rule of thumb is to allow a ten- to twenty-minute cushion in anticipation of unforeseen circumstances. If we encounter no surprises, this extra time can be used to prepare, collect ourselves, and relax. What good is it to compound the misfortune of being late for an event or encounter by interacting without the full possession of our mental, emotional, and sensate faculties? If we discover that our cushion was insufficient, we can compensate for this in the future, or if we feel that our delay was due to rare circumstances, we can simply relax as much as possible, and make the best of the situation.

Punctuality as Communication

Our attitude toward promptness projects an image to others. Habitual tardiness communicates immaturity, discourtesy toward others, or incompetence. Punctuality gets our encounters off to a good start; we never know how our tardiness might affect those with whom we interact. They may interpret our tardiness as symbolic of a lack of professionalism and courtesy, and assume that we are disorganized and unreliable. We cannot control the projections people make about us, but we can influence the data we provide them. A commitment to punctuality is a proactive approach to relationships and activities that yields positive first impressions and unencumbered beginnings.

Conclusion

Punctuality is crucial in providing initial impressions both in business and personal affairs. It communicates competence, courtesy, and integrity, which we can either build upon or tear down in subsequent interactions. It gets us off to a good start, and projects a harmony between our words and deeds that is very important in today's climate of mistrust and superficiality. The requisite self-discipline and planning is a small price to pay for the benefits and positive side effects it provides.

Punctuality is a virtue that avoids the extremes of laxity and scrupulosity. To enhance our likelihood of punctuality, we can estimate the amount of transit or preparation time needed for an encounter or commitment, and allow a cushion to account for deviations attributable to underestimation of transit time or unforeseen circumstances. Rather than view the resulting interim time as downtime, we can treat it as additional preparation or relaxation time. A time cushion helps us avoid unnecessary stress by reducing time pressures.

From both a short-term and long-term perspective, punctuality is an effective and healthy alternative to cutting things close and setting ourselves up for stress and frustration. Who among us is too busy to provide a time cushion that can help preserve our composure, energy, and effectiveness?

In the final chapter of this book, we enter the "cool-down" phase of our journey by reflecting on the importance of rest, relaxation, and recreation as they relate to the art of Personal Energy Management.

Punctuality Pointers

1. Punctuality is a courtesy both to self and others.
    a. Our attitude toward punctuality and the respect we accord other people's time is a message that we communicate.
    b. People can interpret tardiness in a variety of ways that have little to do with reality. In our image-conscious world, punctuality is very expedient.

2. Last-minute beating of the clock provides a momentary stimulus, either positive or negative, and an eventual negative result, stress.
   a. Most people perform worse under pressure, although the surge of adrenaline can be a temporary stimulant to better performance.
   b. Sometimes, due to unforeseen circumstances, you cannot beat the clock.
   c. Plan to be early by giving yourself a cushion. Take advantage of the leftover cushion by using the interim time for a physical, emotional, mental, or spiritual purpose, including simply relaxing and enjoying the present situation. This is the opposite of killing time.

3. Evaluate the importance of punctuality in any given situation. What are the drawbacks from late or premature arrival?
   a. Chronic premature arrival can be discourteous and embarrassing to others.
   b. If the drawbacks from tardiness are considerable, visualize the negative results as a deterrent to any tendency to dawdle or be lax in preparation.

4. Turn punctuality into a personal commitment and challenge. Make it a goal.
   a. Give yourself small incentives or rewards (if only verbal self-congratulations) for being punctual.
   b. Plan departure times by anticipating and factoring in the routine tasks you need to accomplish prior to departing.
   c. For morning meetings or events, always get ready the night before, when you can think clearly and are less likely to forget something.
   d. Visualize yourself getting to work, events, or encounters on time in a relaxed state.

5. Reasonable time constraints can elevate performance. Excessive time and material resources can lull us into carelessness and inefficiency.

6. The following are common roots of tardiness:
    a. An overcrowded schedule (unrealistic expectations as to what can be accomplished in a given time period);
    b. Perfectionism or scrupulosity (the compulsion to do just one last thing before leaving);
    c. Inefficiency;
    d. Habits or behavior patterns, possibly formed in childhood or adolescence, or through the influence of an environment or culture;
    e. Misdirected or repressed emotions. Tardiness can be an expression of anger or a form of rebellion.

Reflection Exercises

Can I identify any patterns of tardiness that I might address by building a time cushion into my schedule?

Are there any attitude adjustments or practical steps I can take to improve my punctuality?

If chronic tardiness is an issue for me, what could be at its roots? The Punctuality Pointers list cites several possibilities: overcrowded schedule, perfectionism, inefficiency, habit, repressed emotions, and rebellion.

What rewards can I offer myself for being punctual?

Which personal experiences have reinforced the importance of punctuality?

Reflections, Applications, and Little Victories

4

Rediscovering the Gift of Leisure

The Art of Energy Conservation

Wasting time seems to have attained the status of a taboo practice in Western culture. It is perceived as unproductive, and productivity is a primary value of a materialistic culture. We are worth what we produce. The tangible aspects of life have been given a higher priority in our cultural value system than the intangible aspects, such as the human virtues.

Why has it not dawned on us that some degree of so-called time wasting is in fact energy regeneration and emotional restoration? Just being for a while helps us produce more effectively when it counts. The principle is similar to that of body-building. The strain of weight lifting tires down muscle tissue, and rest enables it to heal and rebuild. Similarly, our energy and emotion "muscles" need time to heal and develop.

Wasting time must be distinguished from laziness or lethargy, whereby energy and emotion "muscles" get flabby from lack of use. Wasting time is a problem only when its timing is inappropriate or when it becomes chronic and habitual. In moderate proportions, what we refer to as time wasting may not be that at all. Let us examine some therapeutic and creative ways of enjoying leisure.

Carving Out Leisure Time

When was the last time you sat down and spent time with a friend or loved one, without a tight schedule and precise agenda? When did you last make the effort to soak in nature in a relaxed and contemplative manner? Does the clock merely influence and place boundaries on your relaxation time, or are you governed and preoccupied by it? How often do you take a minute or two to say something nice to someone who otherwise might not hear an encouraging word all day?

Reading, various forms of entertainment, edifying or enjoyable conversations, and personal hobbies are legitimate outlets for quality and quantity time allocations. There is a difference between such recreative activities and wasting time. Time is wasted when we lose respect and responsibility for our use of it. Ultimately, we are the best judges of what is a waste of time for us. Unless we are overly lax or apathetic, we usually know when enough is enough. There will be times when we overdo our rest and recreation indulgence, but we can easily exercise damage control through prudence and poise. Our feelings, intuition, practicalities, and reason will let us know when it is time to get back to work.

Rest, Relaxation, and Recreation

Rest, relaxation, and recreation used to be a given in society. Individuals and institutions recognized the importance of balancing work with play, even though the hours spent working may have been longer due to necessity. In our hectic culture, with its bias toward achievement and activity at the expense of contemplation and being, the three Rs may be more important than ever.

Past cultures recognized the importance of rest both for religious and therapeutic purposes, and diligently safeguarded the weekly day of rest known as the *Sabbath*. In recent decades, consumer, political, and commercial forces have joined hands to strip away the aura of respect that once surrounded the Sabbath. The freedom that consumer advocates and business interests fought for brought increased stress and divisive effects on family and community life. Many businesspeople and organizations no longer view work on the Sabbath as an intrusion into personal time, and have developed consciences insensitive to the legitimate human needs of their employees. The short-term benefits of increased productivity are given priority over the long-term cost of employee turnover, morale, and health issues. Because of the lost rest and recreation that excessive overtime entails it is doubtful that this extra activity increases effectiveness in the long run.

Observing a day or period of rest does not confine us to inactivity or inertia, but to a break from the cycle of frantic activity that characterizes the rest of our week. Certain intense and draining tasks can be deferred to another day, while necessary chores such as cooking or cleaning can be performed in a relaxed and pleasant manner. An excellent source for reflection on the primacy of the Sabbath is Abraham Joshua Heschel's classic, *The Sabbath*. Rabbi Heschel's differentiation of existence between time and space helps us recognize how we can become consumed with space (that is, *doing* and material progress) at the expense of time (that is, *being* and the quality of life). The Sabbath is a day to remind us of God's primacy, and help us get our lives in balance and moderation.

Modern culture's emphasis on production and achievement has led to material and medical advances, but not necessarily whole-person health improvements. As evidenced by the proliferation of violence, frenzy, and discord in today's world, one could assert that these advances have been accompanied by a disturbing devaluation of the human values of rest, relaxation, and recreation. Positive responses to these trends have arisen in the form of increased interest in spirituality, wellness, and community health, but these exceed the scope of our study. We shall be content to reflect upon the benefits of rest, relaxation, and recreation, while considering what we can do to develop their presence and efficacy in our lives.

Rest

It is no secret that for many people sufficient sleep has lost its priority and status as a necessity. Without passing judgment on individual situations, it is important to state the following: Sufficient amounts of sleep are necessary for human health and effectiveness. While the amount of sleep sufficient for health and effectiveness varies with the individual and circumstance, there are certain minimum standards that scientists and doctors point to as guidelines. You can borrow sleeping time temporarily, but you eventually have to pay it back.

If we are tired, stressed, or depressed, we may be getting too much or too little sleep. In such cases we would be wise to consult a health care professional. From the personal growth and effectiveness perspective of this book, we can state that we cannot channel our energies, emotions, and abilities in the proper direction and manner if we do not have the requisite sleep and rest to recharge our batteries. The acid test of rest is how we feel, act, and look. Getting a proper amount of rest is a fundamental element of Personal Energy Management that should not be compromised in order to fit more into our day. If our day is too crowded, we must eliminate the dispensable, rather than the essential, activities.

Relaxation

It is easy in today's activist world to forget the true meaning of relaxation. Advertisers would have us think it means going off on a luxury cruise to a secluded tropical isle, or sitting down to a cold beer. In a very holistic sense, *relaxation* means to let go, to release tension. Relaxation is giving our mental, spiritual, emotional, and physical muscles a break. Relaxation is *being* as well as *doing*.

Why is relaxation so hard for us? One reason seems to be that we are so used to judging ourselves by tangible and material results that we have unconsciously devalued passive or receptive activities, subordinating them to more productive enterprises. It is difficult for us to sit still because we think the world and life will pass us by.

Excessive emphasis on material possessions, tangible results, and practical achievements gives us more things to live with, and less time and capacity to enjoy them. Most religions and philosophies contain valuable wisdom and techniques for slowing down and centering on such basics of life as our body, breath, heartbeat, and being. There are innumerable self-help books from a wellness and personal growth standpoint that offer various breathing exercises and methods of meditation. Our objective is to state that relaxation is part of our vocation. One of the original reasons for the institution of the Sabbath was so that the Israelites would recognize that the world did not rest entirely on their shoulders. If God could rest on the Sabbath, so could they. How we relax depends on the individual. As with rest and recreation, the quality of our relaxation is reflected in how we feel, look, and respond once we re-enter the world of activity.

We do not need to retreat to a tropical paradise to relax. We can relax in a car amid an otherwise frustrating traffic jam. We can focus on pleasant, rather than anxious, thoughts. We can relax by a fire with a loved one. We can listen to music we enjoy, or bury ourselves in a good book. We can relieve tension by weeding out peripheral activities that drain and frustrate us. We can try to discover a still point or place in our lives where we can suspend temporarily our cares and anxieties, and center ourselves on important issues and values. Relaxation is fun, healthy, and effective, and we do not need an excuse or permission.

Recreation

Recreation is *re-creation;* it recharges our batteries. All work and no play makes us dull and bored human beings. An important element of recreation is humor, defined as the capacity to be amused and enthused by life. Are we not entitled to enjoy ourselves through a hobby, short or extended vacation, social gathering, or an enjoyable pastime? The Contemplation, Leisure, and Humor Checklist at the end of this chapter offers a sampling of such activities and pastimes.

Although the joyless and macho attitudes of materialism (that is, things take precedence over people) and consumerism plague our society, they cannot take away the will to be human and to enjoy the good things in life. The bad things will be there whether we enjoy ourselves or not; why not enjoy the good things while we can? What better way to end our reflections than to renew our appreciation of the good things in life, and to affirm, in what for many of us is a valiant act of courage and faith, that life *is* worth *living!*

Contemplation, Leisure, and Humor Checklist

When was the last time you:
- ❑ Sat down for three minutes to take deep, relaxing breaths, perhaps using your breathing pattern to regain your composure under stress . . .
- ❑ Consciously enjoyed the quiet around you, actually immersing yourself in it . . .
- ❑ While driving a car, stepped back from a rushed experience to simply observe people, places, and things around you . . .
- ❑ Used an awareness exercise to get in touch with your senses . . .
- ❑ Took time out of your day to refocus and center yourself in silence . . .
- ❑ Used quiet to help you sort out your priorities and address only the most pressing duties . . .
- ❑ Listened to your heart in silence, responding in a small, practical way . . .
- ❑ Recorded your thoughts and feelings in a journal . . .
- ❑ Repeated affirmations or visualizations in silence . . .
- ❑ Expressed your feeling to God in an honest dialogue . . .
- ❑ Shared silence with friends or family . . .
- ❑ Read an inspirational passage, poem, or book . . .
- ❑ Enjoyed light, soothing, calming music either alone or with company . . .
- ❑ Enjoyed a nonintense evening with someone when you simply relaxed, were yourself, and perhaps traded enjoyable stories, anecdotes, or remembrances . . .
- ❑ Played a fun game where you could let your hair down and cut loose . . .
- ❑ Made an effort to lift your spirits by thinking affirming thoughts . . .

❑ Tried simply enjoying people, or a particular person, for who they are, rather than analyzing or criticizing them (or worst of all, trying to change them) . . .

❑ Reflected on the absurd nature of puffed-up, self-important behavior, rather than get angry at it . . .

❑ Used your imagination to conjure absurd, ironic, and incongruent images (for example, an intoxicated moose ballerina or a dog trying to catch a wave) . . .

❑ Gently reflected on your own intensity and how trivial some of the things that upset you are . . .

❑ Experienced a good comedy act, movie, show, or television program . . .

❑ Budgeted time in your day for a fun, relaxing, recreative activity . . .

❑ Took a nice long walk and enjoyed the fresh air . . .

❑ Observed your lovable imperfection and fondly laughed at yourself . . .

❑ Observed the tragic comedy and irony of everyday life circumstances . . .

❑ Rented an enjoyable video, perhaps with friends or family . . .

❑ Took a day or weekend trip to be with nature . . .

❑ Listened to music that speaks to your heart and perhaps evokes happy memories . . .

❑ Indulged yourself in a relaxing hobby or pastime . . .

❑ Permitted yourself to take a day off from your busy schedule for play purposes . . .

❑ Read an entertaining book or story . . .

❑ Spent time in relaxing, nostalgic conversation with friends or family . . .

❑ Affirmed yourself for making a silly mistake that you could learn from . . .

Reflection Exercises

Do I get sufficient sleep? If not, how can I modify my schedule or address insomnia-related issues to ensure the necessary rest?

Do I allocate sufficient time, energy, and financial resources for recreation?

When I recreate, do I worry about work or even the recreation activity itself? Does an element of pressure or competition seep in, or am I able to just relax? If not, what corrective or therapeutic measures could I take?

Do I observe a day or periodic time of rest? Can I identify the fruit of my practice or neglect?

Personal Experiences of Contemplation, Leisure, and Humor

Further Reading

Amaldas, Swami. *Christian Yogic Meditation*. Wilmington, Del.: Michael Glazier, 1983.

Assagioli, Roberto. *The Act of Will*. Baltimore, Md.: Penguin Books, 1974.

Beck, Aaron T. "Cognitive Therapy." *Behavior Therapy* 1 (1970): 184–200.

————. *Depression*. New York: Harper, 1967.

————. *Love Is Never Enough*. New York: Harper and Row, 1988.

Burns, David D. *Feeling Good: The New Mood Therapy*. New York: Signet, 1980.

————. *The Feeling Good Handbook*. New York: Plume, 1990.

del Mazza, Valentino. *The Patience of God*. Boston, Mass.: St. Paul Books and Media, 1985.

Dwyer, Vincent, O.C.S.O. *Lift Your Sails: The Challenge of Being a Christian*. New York: Doubleday, 1987.

Edman, David. *Your Weaknesses Are Your Strengths*. Chicago, Ill.: Loyola University Press, 1994.

Ellis, Albert, and Robert Harper. *A New Guide to Rational Living*. North Hollywood, Ca.: Wilshire Book Company, 1975.

Frankl, Viktor E. *Man's Search for Meaning*. New York: Washington Square Press, 1984.

————. *The Unheard Cry for Meaning: Psychotherapy and Humanism*. New York: Washington Square Press, 1978.

————. *The Will to Meaning: Foundations and Applications of Logotherapy*. New York: Meridian, 1988.

Furey, Robert. *So I'm Not Perfect*. New York: Alba House, 1986.

Furlong, Monica. *Thérèse of Lisieux*. New York: Pantheon, 1987.

Ganss, George, S.J., trans. *The Spiritual Exercises of Saint Ignatius*. Chicago: Loyola University Press, 1992.

Grassi, Joseph. *Changing the World Within*. New York: Paulist Press, 1986.

———. *Healing the Heart*. New York: Paulist Press, 1987.

Hall, Brian P. *The Genesis Effect*. Mahwah, N.J.: Paulist Press, 1986.

Hansel, Tim. *When I Relax I Feel Guilty*. Elgin, Ill.: David C. Cook Publishing, 1979.

Helmstetter, Shad. *The Self-Talk Solution*. New York: Pocket Books, 1987.

Heschel, Abraham Joshua. *The Sabbath*. New York: Noonday Press, 1951.

Hughes, Louis. *Body Mind and Spirit*. Mystic, Conn.: Twenty-Third Publications, 1991.

Keating, Thomas. *Invitation to Love*. Rockport, Mass.: Element Books, 1992.

Lakein, Alan. *How to Get Control of Your Time and Your Life*. New York: Signet, 1973.

Lisieux, Thérèse of. *Autobiography of a Saint: The Story of a Soul*. Trans. Ronald Knox. London: Fontana, 1960.

Martini, Carlo Maria. *Perseverance in Trials*. Collegeville, Minn.: Liturgical Press, 1992.

May, Gerald. *Addiction and Grace*. San Francisco: Harper, 1988.

———. *Simply Sane*. New York: Crossroad, 1993.

Michael, Chester, and Marie Norrisey. *Arise*. Charlottesville, Va.: Open Door, 1981.

Nimeth, Rev. Albert. *Thoughts for Reflection*. Boston, Mass.: St. Paul Books and Media, 1986.

Powell, John. *The Christian Vision*. Allen, Tex.: Argus Communications, 1984.

———. *Happiness Is an Inside Job*. Allen, Tex.: Tabor, 1989.

Schultz, Karl A. *The Art and Vocation of Caring for Persons in Pain*. Mahwah, N.J.: Paulist Press, 1993.

———. *Journaling with Moses and Job*. Boston, Mass.: St. Paul Books and Media, 1995.

———. *Where Is God When You Need Him?: Sharing Stories of Suffering with Job and Jesus*. Staten Island, N.Y.: Alba House, 1992.

Scott, Dru. *How to Put More Time in Your Life.* New York: Signet, 1980.

Suenens, Cardinal Leon-Joseph. *Nature and Grace.* Ann Arbor, Mich.: Servant Books, 1985.

Tweedie, Donald F. *Logotherapy and the Christian Faith: An Evaluation of Frankl's Existential Approach to Psychotherapy.* Grand Rapids, Mich.: Baker Book House, 1961.

van Kaam, Adrian. *Living Creatively.* Denville, N.J.: Dimension Books, 1972.

Vitz, Paul C. *Psychology as Religion.* Grand Rapids, Mich.: Wm. B. Eerdmans, 1977.